U0051116

大旗出版
BANNER PUBLISHING

大旗出版
BANNER PUBLISHING

馬力歐（Marion Erskine）◎著　陳怡良◎繪

Dear Marion Erskine

It is with a sense of great humility and happiness that I wish to congratulate you for taking the time to write this wonderful book on South Africa and Taiwan.

It is amazing how the South African and Taiwanese cultural diversity differs from each other.

The cultural activities of a nation are an experience of an intense impulse to externalize ourselves, through creative activities by means of which we respect, comment, critique and ponder the human condition. They are also experience of our lives as an animal species endowed with a host of creative powers.

It is through cultural activity that we proclaim and assert our identities. It is through these activities as well that we affirm our common humanity, which though extremely diverse has discovered the means of communicating its deepest emotions and passion.

It is my sincere hope that all those who are going to read this book may be inspired by what the writer had produced.

Petrus Meyer
Head of Mission
Liaison Office of the Republic
of South Africa in Taipei Taiwan

親愛的馬力歐：

　　非常榮幸也相當高興，在殷殷期盼之下，恭喜你寫的這本關於南非與台灣的書籍終於順利出版。

　　書中，你娓娓道來所有關於南非與台灣、西方與東方之間文化的差異與多變性，我相當驚訝，這兩者間竟是如此的不同。

　　一個國家的文化活動，是該國人民的自我需求所產生出的一種具體回應。透過創作，以及其他新的呈現方式，讓我們尊重、了解、質疑，甚至是思考以及省思身為人類一份子所應盡的義務與責任。而這些文化體驗，同時也是上天賦予人類，之所以成為萬物之首的原因。

　　藉由這些文化活動，使我們再次清楚地表明和確信我們的個人特質，同時也證實身為人類的通性，那就是，所有的溝通與思想交流，都是來自心靈最深處的情感與熱情。

　　我真誠的希望那些閱讀過本書的人們，能從作者幽默的文筆中得到一些激勵和啟發。

南非共和國駐台辦事處 代表

梅逸伯

　　我在台灣第一個南非式的烤肉聚會上認識了Marion，他給我的感覺就像是一個很有使命感的人，而且毫不猶豫地告訴我台灣有多棒，還有關於他在這裡的一切經驗的書籍。

　　我很佩服Marion還有他的台灣夥伴藝術家Jasyn。對台灣而言，這將是第一本，而且是一本非常獨特書，使用單一語言出版一本書是個挑戰，但是用兩種語言，加上插圖！很明顯的這兩個有才華的年輕人其創造力正在一路攀升。

　　這本書並不像是典型的西方人觀點，Marion熱愛台灣的程度讓我覺得他像是個披著外國人皮膚的台灣人，有時幽默，有時嚴肅，但總是保有著敏銳的觸感，這本書讓讀者深入了解一個外國人在另一個和自己背景截然不同的文化裡，有趣卻又真實的生活。

　　小心囉！不論你讀的是中文版還是英文版本，這些年輕的新星已經證明了他們的才能，我很確定這本書決不會是他們唯一的一部作品！

I met Marion at my first South African barbeque in Taiwan. He struck me as a man with a mission and didn't hesitate to tell me how fantastic Taiwan is, and about his book chronicling his experiences here.

I was impressed, both with Marion and his Taiwanese co-artist, Jasyn.

This book truly is remarkably unique and must be a first for Taiwan. Publishing a book in one language is a challenge, but in two, with illustrations, drives home the point that these talented young men are just on the base of an upward creativity curve.

Reading the book, what is immediately obvious, is that this isn't really a typical Westerners perspective. Marion has embraced Taiwan and her people with such passion that he appears to me as a Taiwanese in Western skin. Sometimes humorous, sometimes serious, but always with sensitivity, this book gives readers real but funny insights into a foreigner's life, in a culture so remarkably different from our own.

Watch out, these bright young stars have done themselves proud, no matter whether you are reading the Chinese or the English. I'm positive this will not be the last we see of them!

Marcelle

　　謹以這本書獻給在台灣的所有人，包括本地人以及外來客，同時也獻給所有想要拜訪台灣的人。

　　橫跨東西方之間的文化橋樑或許相當大，即使今日我們的世界經由高科技和文化的迅速傳播已經逐漸縮小，但對東西方來說，彼此的文化景象仍是十分新鮮。

　　在本書中，我很樂意將我初次拜訪台灣的經驗分享給大家，讓您可以發現外國人眼中的台灣究竟是怎樣的一幅光景，以及我們來台灣之前，對台灣的認知和彼此文化之間的差異。有時一些翻譯上的誤解是無法避免的，相信所有的外國人都有一大堆類似的故事可以告訴你，然而，我希望可以藉由這本書讓這兩個不同文化的東西方世界更加靠近。

　　台灣讓我成長、蛻變成一個更好的人，所以我想藉著這個機會與世界各地的人分享我令人難忘的經驗。

　　歡迎加入我們的旅程！

This book is dedicated to all the people in Taiwan, both indigenous and foreign, as well as to anyone who is interested in coming here.

Probably the biggest cultural bridge to cross is that between West and East, and although our world is getting smaller and smaller due to faster technology and cultures flying to and fro, it is still a very new cultural landscape to both sides.

In this book, I would like to share my first experiences in Taiwan with you all. How do foreigners see this island? What do we know of Taiwan before we come here? How different is their culture really from our own?

Being 'lost in translation' is inevitable and all of us have a few stories to tell. With this book, I hope I can bring these two cultures closer together.

Taiwan has really changed me into a better person, and I want to take this opportunity to share this amazing experience with you and the world.

Welcome, to my JOURNEY!

Marion Erskine

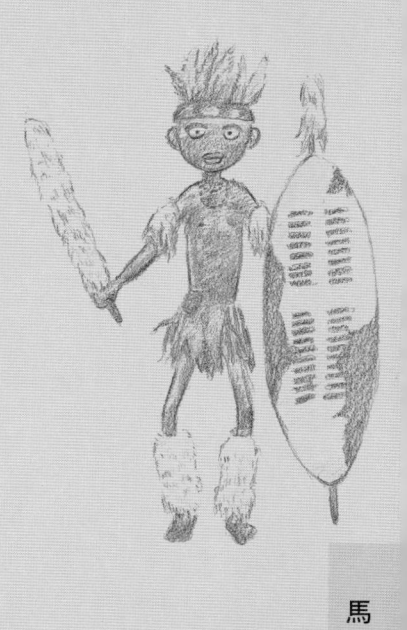

Foreword

馬力歐帶你瘋台灣

009

繪序

啥! 我也要寫序!!
What! I need to write a foreword, too!!

比較優越?
Superiority?

比較獨立?
Independence?

阿度仔

比較大?
Bigger?

比較有錢?
Rich?

我想很多人
都跟我一樣
對於這些外來客充滿
好奇心
他們是怎樣的人
他們在台灣
過著怎樣
的生活?

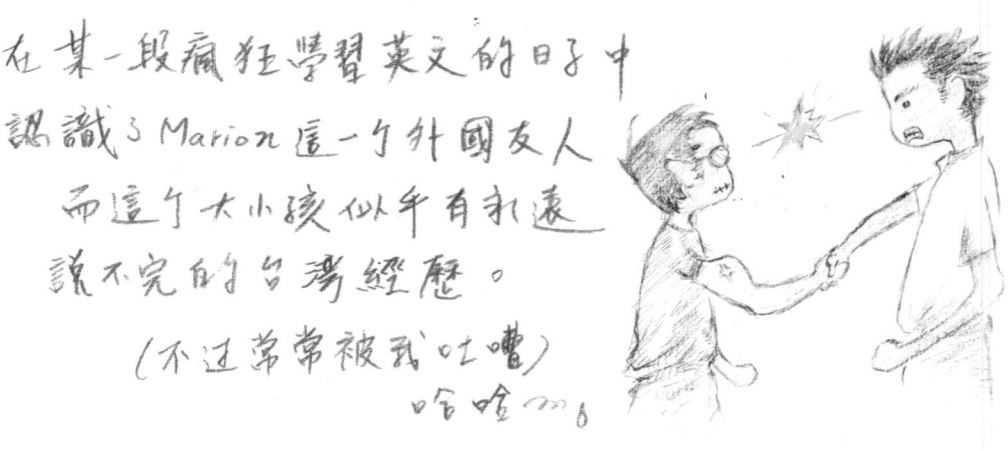

在某一段瘋狂學習英文的日子中
認識了Marion這个外國友人
而這个大小孩似乎有永遠
說不完的台灣經歷。
(不过常常被我吐嘈)
哈哈

從他的眼中
著實讓人看到了
一个不一樣的
台灣

有時當我們住在一个地方太久
　往往會讓人忽略身邊的事物
　也許藉由一个外國人的眼中、思想
　正能提醒我們該珍惜周遭
　平常不會留意到的寶藏

yummy!

準備好沒？
　就讓我們一起分享
　　住在台灣的另一种聲音

It doesn't matter whether you are a Taiwanese
or a foreigner, I hope we all live life to the fullest
and enjoy this beautiful island.
　　　　Together. Forever.

双極魚
Jasyn

目 錄 CONTENTS

01

一切由此開始

It all begins here

　　我來自於非洲大陸南端的國家──南非，它不只是一個有著令人屏息美景的國家。在這片土地上，更有著迥異的種族文化與景色，而這讓它成為著名的「彩虹國度」──將不同的世界融合在一個國家之中。

　　在我們的國家裡有許多不同的種族與語言，光是正式的官方語言就高達11種之多。不論你的膚色是白的、黑的、褐色或是亞洲人，在這個黑暗又閃著鑽石光芒的非洲國度裡，人們都能和諧的住在一起，而且在廢除種族隔離政策之後，我們也日漸有一個共同的新認知，那就是我們都可以很驕傲地稱自己為「非洲人」。

I am from the spectacular and beautiful country, South Africa, right at the tip of Africa. South Africa is not just breathtakingly beautiful, but is also so diverse in cultures and landscapes, that it is known as the 'Rainbow Nation', an 'eclectic world in one country'.

Our Rainbow Nation consists of many different Ethnic groups and believe it or not, we have eleven official languages.

Black, White, Brown and Asian live together in harmony in this diamond of the Dark Continent and day-by-day we build on a new identity after breaking the terrible chains of our apartheid past. Although we are, all from different cultural backgrounds, we are all proud to be called "African".

2

　　南非有著多變的景觀，從聳入雲端的高山一直到綿延千里，無止無盡的平原，你都可以一覽無遺。在東半部，我們有熱帶森林與香蕉種植園；在西半部，我們卻有著炎熱的沙漠。另一個令人驚嘆的地標便是位於開普敦（Cape Town）的桌山（Table Mountain），它的獨特，為這個港市造就了令人稱羨的風景，也使得開普敦成為世界上最美麗的城市之一。

　　Our checkered landscapes range from high mountains that stretch into the clouds to flat lands that run for miles without end. We have tropical forests with banana plantations in the eastern side and hot deserts on the western side. An amazing landmark is Table Mountain that towers above the city of Cape Town. This truly distinguishable mountain creates a breathtaking background to this harbor city and many say that it is by far one of the most beautiful cities in the world.

壯觀的植物和野生生物造就了南非的獨一無二
我們有眾所周知的5大野生動物
包括獅子、犀牛、大象、獵豹和水牛

One of the things that makes my country
unique is the amazing plant and wildlife. We
have the 'Big 5' as it is known, which consists
of the lion, the rhino, the elephant, the cheetah
and the buffalo.

壯觀的植物和野生生物造就了南非的獨一無二。
我們有眾所周知的5大野生動物，包括獅子、犀牛、
大象、獵豹和水牛。這些動物確確實實是非洲的資
產，我們非常驕傲能有專屬的自然環境和生態來保護
牠們。我們讓這些動物在野外恣意奔馳，厭惡看見牠
們被關在動物園堅固的牢籠之中。沒有什麼比得上一
趟真正的野外之旅，在這裡，你可以坐在敞開的吉普
車上觀看動物們棲息的自然環境，目睹獵豹以最高速
度奔跑，或者看著獅子獵捕牠的下一餐，這些風景完
完全全令人悸動與驚嘆。

One of the things that makes my country
unique is the amazing plant and wildlife. We have
the 'Big 5' as it is known, consisting of the lion, the
rhino, the elephant, the cheetah and the buffalo.
These animals are all truly African and we are very
proud to protect them in our wildlife and nature
reserves. We are so spoiled to see these animals
running free in the wild and hate going to zoos
where animals are caged up behind thick bars.
There is nothing like a real wildlife safari where you
drive in an open jeep and see the animals as they
live in their natural environment. It's breathtaking
to see a cheetah running at full speed or a lion
hunting for its next meal.

我們國家的英雄納爾遜曼德拉（Nelson Mandela）也是舉世聞名。他於90年代早期獲得釋放，夢想是創造一個沒有偏見和腐敗統治的國家，而他也因此贏得了諾貝爾和平獎。在打破種族隔離政策的這個枷鎖之後，全世界都等著看我們國家的變化。然而，在所有南非人堅定的決心之下，無論信念和背景的差異，一個完善的民主制度由此而生。

像所有國家一樣，我們也有我們的問題，愛滋病就是社會中極需解決的重大問題。由於缺乏完善的教育，疾病的傳播與感染非常迅速，這是我們必須要面對的最大障礙，而高犯罪率也是南非每日必須應付的主要挫折課題。但即使有這些問題必須面對，南非的經濟仍是持續成長，而每一個南非人也堅決貫徹這個夢想。

Our country's national hero, Nelson Mandela is also well-known to everyone in the world. Nelson Mandela was released in the 1992 and his dream was to have a nation where no prejudice and corruption ruled. He won the Nobel Peace prize for this exact dream. After his release, the whole world waited anxiously to see what would happen to my country. Yet, there was an undeterred determination from all South Africans, no matter what creed or background to build up our country, and from this a wonderful democracy was born.

Like all countries, we do have our fare share of problems, with HIV/Aids being one of the main concerns within our society. Due to the lack of good education, the disease has left millions of people infected and this is one of the biggest obstacles we have to face. Crime is also a major setback that people have to deal with on a daily basis. However, even with all of our problems, South Africa's economy is improving and people are determined to make it work.

納爾遜曼德拉（Nelson Mandela）

南非不只是你記憶中的一個尋常國家，我們確實成功應證了，即使是不同宗教、文化和語言的人也是可以融洽相處在一起，甚至可以提升至更高層次的一個國家。擁有這個世界上所有人種、展現出他們的不同面孔，使得彩虹國度並非浪得虛名。

這就是南非，我的家鄉，我的根，我將在這本書中和大家一起分享我的夢想、我的經歷以及我的人生。

South Africa isn't just your average country. We are a nation which is actually succeeding in proving that different religions, cultures and languages can actually work together and can influence people to greater heights. Having all the ethnic colors of the world represented through the faces of our people, we are not called the 'Rainbow Nation' for nothing.

So this is where I am from. These are my roots. And in this book, I'm going to share my dreams, my experiences and my life with you all.

02 叫台灣的島嶼
The island called Taiwan

　　仍記得小時候我經常一個人獨自玩玩具，而且一玩就是好幾個小時，因為豐富的想像力讓我不需要跟很多朋友一起玩耍也可以感到快樂，而且我發現自己最快樂的時光便是和想像力及玩具悠閒地待在房間裡。

　　有一天當我盡情玩耍時，翻轉了其中一個玩具，在它的底部發現一行字：「MADE IN TAIWAN」。好奇的我立刻轉了轉我所有的玩具，結果所有我最喜愛的玩具中都印有「MADE IN TAIWAN」的字樣，這時我馬上衝去找正在廚房準備午餐的媽媽。

　　「媽咪，台灣在哪裡啊？」我問著。

　　「嗯……兒子，它在遙遠的東方，一個離這裡非常、非常遙遠的地方。」她看起來有點疑惑。

　　「你為什麼問這個呢？」媽媽微笑地問著。

　　「因為我所有最酷的玩具都是從那裡來的！」我滿臉笑容地回答了她。

　　這是我對台灣的第一個印象，而當我終於在地圖上看見了這個島嶼，我不敢相信，這麼小的地方居然製造出那麼多好玩的東西，這讓我不禁深深著迷。

I can still remember as a child how I used to play with my toys for hours and hours. I always kept myself busy with my toys and I was happiest when I could play alone.

One day I played with my toys. I turned one over and it said "MADE IN TAIWAN" at the bottom of the toy. I immediately turned all my toys around. It was printed on every single of my favorite toys! I rushed to the kitchen where my mother was preparing lunch.

"Mom, where is Taiwan?" I asked her.

"Well, my son. It's in the Far East. Very very far from here."

She looked puzzled.

"Why do you ask?" she asked me with a smile.

"Because all my cool toys are from there!"

And that's how I first heard about Taiwan. When I eventually saw this small island on a map, I couldn't believe that so many nice things were made in a small place like this. I was fascinated.

　　我對小孩子們一直有股熱忱，想要幫助他們，並且教導他們成為一個更好、更有用的人；想給予他們一個更好的自我形象，讓他們為這苛刻的世界做好準備。這也是為什麼我決定要成為一位老師，我主修英語和南非荷蘭語（一種南非語言，相當類似荷蘭語），而在我拿到了高等教育教學文憑之後，我便投入了教育的領域。

　　同時，我也非常著迷於旅行。我遊歷過許多國家，而在一次美國旅遊期間，無意間聽到一個可以來台灣教學機會。台灣？不就是那個製造出很多精細又好玩的玩具的地方嗎？這立刻引起了我的興趣，我一直很想到遙遠的東方國度旅行，當然，不只是因為它製造出很多好玩的玩具，也因為我一直對這個和我文化背景、生活方式完全不同的地方心醉神馳。

　　所以，在 2002 年我做了一個重大的決定，那就是前去征服遙遠的東方。於是，我搭上了飛機，帶著我唯一會的二個中文字「您好」，啟程航向台灣，並開始了我的冒險旅途。

啦啦……我來了台灣！

Cause I'm leaving on a jetplane.. Don't know when I'll be back again…

All through my life, I've always had a passion for children. To help them and teach them and make better people of them. I've always wanted to give them good self-images and prepare them for the harsh world out there. This is also the reason why I decided to study to become a teacher. I majored in English and Afrikaans (a South African language quite similar to Dutch) as well as other subjects. I completed a diploma in Higher Education teaching, afterwich I entered the world of education.

I've traveled to many places in the world and during a journey in the United States, I heard of the possibility to teach in Taiwan. Taiwan?! The place which always made such nice toys? I was immediately interested. I've always liked the idea of traveling to the Far East, because that is the place that's so far from my civilization and the way that we do things.

So, in 2002 I decided to take a big step to conquer the Far East. I got on an airplane, and I set off to Taiwan with only two words in my vocabulary: "Ni hao!"

03

您好！高雄
Hello Kaohsiung

一切都像是昨天才剛發生的一樣。在六月份一個寒冷的冬天，我從約翰尼斯堡搭上了往台灣的飛機，帶著一件厚重的外套，我渾然忘記這個即將要著陸的新城市——高雄，是處在另一個季節和時區的地方。

通過海關後，突然明白自己和其他人看起來有多不一樣，我有190公分高耶！而我週遭都是亞洲面孔，而且各個都比我矮。我環顧四週發現到很少有寫著英文的標誌，我不禁問自己到底做了一個什麼樣的決定，突然感到害怕了起來，但同時也感到一股莫名的興奮。

I can still remember it like yesterday. I climbed onto an airplane in Johannesburg in June. It was winter and freezing cold and I had an extra jacket with me. When I climbed out of that airplane in Kaohsiung, I forgot that I was in a new season and a new time zone.

I walked through customs and realized that no-one looked like me. Everybody was Asian and short. I am 190cm tall. There was no signage in English and I said to myself: "What have you done!?" I was very excited, but really scared.

穿越人群，我感覺到有很多人一直注視著自己，幾乎所有人看到我都會說出兩個字「Hen Gao」，我不禁納悶那到底是什麼意思？只能繼續前去提領自己的行李，走出機場。

請別誤會！雖然非洲很炎熱，幾乎比世界上所有國家都還要炎熱，但是在抵達台灣的那一天，那潮濕的熱氣幾乎讓我快受不了了，我從來沒有這種感覺，好就像幾乎要淹死在外面那濃稠的濕氣之中。在短短的幾秒鐘裡，我的衣服馬上就黏在皮膚上了，活像是我的第二層肌膚，那感覺就像是正在火焰之上燒烤的肉一樣。

As I walked I saw people looking at me and most of them said two words: "Hen Gao". I thought to myself: "What does that mean?" After I got my bags, I walked outside.

Don't get me wrong. Africa gets very hot. Probably hotter than most places in Europe, but it was the humidity that almost killed me the day I arrived. I've never had this feeling before. It felt like I was drowning outside in the dense humidity. In a matter of seconds my clothes stuck to me like second skin and felt that I was going to go up in flames any second.

幸運地，有一個同樣從南非來的朋友已經在機場等我了，我們搭乘巴士前往高雄市區。在巴士上談話的同時，我的汗水也不停地從指尖上滑落下來，真是熱斃了！而她也告訴我：我們將會坐火車前往我的下一個家「屏東」。

我從巴士的窗口向外望去，一大堆中文字和廣告招牌一個接著一個快速閃過我眼簾，大的、小的、白的、藍的，像是綿延無盡的萬花筒景象一般。我的腦袋試著想要去理解所有的意思，但是我還是無法去看懂它們，漸漸地，我的腦袋就痛了起來。朋友告訴我不要去理會那些，只要在這裡待得夠久，根本就不會注意到它們的存在，我心理想著，要是真的如此，對我來說那可真是一個好消息。

我們下了巴士後便買了前往屏東的火車票。當我提起大行李時，再一次聽到「Hen Gao」，那到底是什麼意思呢？而且有些人跟我擦肩而過之後，還會回過頭來指著我叫「Wei Guo Ren」朋友告訴我那是「外國人」的意思。後來認識了第一個台灣朋友之後，他們告訴我「Hen Gao」就是很高的意思，這終於讓我鬆了一口氣，還好不是什麼不好的稱呼。

Fortunately for me, a friend was there from South Africa and came to meet me. We got onto a bus. As we were talking, the sweat literally dripped from my fingertips. She told me that we were going to take a train to my next home. The city of Pingtung.

I looked outside the bus windows and all I could see were Chinese characters passing by me sign after sign. Big ones, small ones, blue ones, white ones. My brain immediately tried to make sense of all of this and I was unable to read anything. I started getting a headache right away. My friend told me to just ignore them and gave me some advice: "Ignore them. If you're here long enough, you won't even notice them anymore." That would be really nice, I thought.

We got off the bus and bought tickets for Pingtung. As I carried my huge bags, I heard "Hen Gao" again. What does this mean? People also turned and pointed... shouting the word "Wei Guo Ren" as we were walking past them. My friend told me that the last word meant 'foreigner'. It was only after I met my first Taiwanese friend, that they translated the "Hen Gao" to 'Very tall!'. I was relieved.

04

蹲還是不蹲？
To Squat or not to Squat

在我的台灣生活裡，有著光彩和不光彩的一天，那發生在我第一次走進廁所，發現一個必須蹲下的馬桶。我聽說過這個在東方世界赫赫有名的馬桶，但是卻衷心的祈禱不會有用到它的一天。在南非，我們壓根兒沒想過會有這種樣子的馬桶，因為我們總是樂於舒舒服服地坐著解決自己的需求。

就在某天，人類的天性來的真的不是時候，地方也相當不對之時，我知道自己再也無法避免這個考驗了。我打開了廁所的門，沒錯！就是它，一個凸出於地面可笑的瓷器正在地面上跟我揮手，我必須有一個方法去使用這個東西，但誰能告訴我要如何做呢？請諒解每一個人都有他的自尊，我可沒有那個膽量走出去，隨便找一個台灣人問他「嘿！朋友！請告訴我如何使用你們這個的馬桶！」

我慢慢地走了進去，做了一個深深的呼吸並且關上門。就是這一天了，我必須要搞懂怎麼使用它。我呆呆的望著它好一陣子，到底要怎麼坐？怎麼站在那上面呢？而褲子要脫到哪裡呢？我一點概念也沒有，不知道會不會搞得一團糟。而到底是該面對著這個凸出來的拱門，還是背對著它？而我該抓住哪裡嗎？我想起以前上體育課

Another (un)exiting day in my life in Taiwan was the first time I walked into the bathroom and found a squatting toilet. I've heard of these notorious toilets in the East, but I prayed that I would never have to use one of these. n South Africa we don't know squat toilets at all and we're much happier sitting comfortably during the performance!

One day, mother nature called in the wrong place at the wrong time, and I knew there was no way out of this situation. I opened the bathroom door and there it was! A funny porcelain hole waving at me from the ground. Today was the day that I had to figure out how this thing worked. But how? Please understand that we all have our pride and I didn't have the boldness to just walk up to a Taiwanese friend and say: "Hey mate, tell me how your toilets work over here".

I walked in slowly, took a deep breath and closed the door behind me. I stared at it for quite a while. How do you mount this thing? How do you stand? How far do your pants have to go down? I don't know!? What if I make a mess? Does the arch thing that sticks out of the ground have to face me or my back? Where do I hold on to? I realized that I hated squats in physical education class too, and now I was forced to do this.

時就很討厭常要蹲著，但是現在又要被迫再一次的去面對它。

　　好吧，事情是這樣的。那時是怎麼會想到要這麼做，到現在我都還不是很清楚。我把褲子脫下到膝蓋的地方，站超過那個坑，並且面對著門，背對著那個半圓形的拱門，希望一切都會進行得很順利。就這樣，我把一隻手放在瓷器打造的拱門上，然後再伸另一隻手張開，並且伸長了雙腳。噔噔！這就是這個笨笨的外國人第一次使用蹲式馬桶的樣子，活像一張人形桌子般，這個動作真的讓我的手酸到了極點，我心想：天啊！這裡的人想必都擁有一對非常強壯的手臂，才可以去使用像這樣的馬桶。最後我非常安全的逃離那裡，並且沒有搞亂任何一點東西，我成功的完成這項可怕的任務，真是為自己感到驕傲，太了不起了！

　　過了幾個禮拜後，我鼓足了勇氣請教了一位朋友到底該如何正確使用它。當我聽到他述說台灣人使用版本後，我實在止不住哈哈大笑，不過我仍然認為這個方法是一個訓練三頭肌非常有效的方式，哈哈……

Okay, here goes. I still don't know how I achieved this, but I lowered my pants to my knees, I stood over the hole, facing the door. The arch was behind me. Let's hope for the best. I reached back and placed my right hand on the porcelain arch, then the left. I spread my legs far and wide, and here was the "stupid foreigner" resembling a human table for his first squatting experience. The pain in my upper arms was extreme and I thought to myself: "Goodness, these people should have amazing arms for being able to do this!" I got out of there quite safely and without making any mess. I successfully completed this dreadful task.

It was weeks later, that I had the boldness to ask a friend how to use a squatter properly. I couldn't stop laughing when I heard his version of the instruction manual to Taiwan Squatters! I still think my way is a great way for working the triceps!

「嘿！朋友！請告訴我如何使用你們這個的馬桶！」
"Hey mate, tell me how your toilets work over here".

05

熟悉的聲音
That Familiar Sound

　　我想在台灣的每一個外國人對於這個故事都有他們自己的版本，但其結尾相信都是同樣的結論，那就是極度的失望。

　　大部分來到東方遊覽的西方拜訪者都會不禁抱怨的便是這裡的炎熱濕氣，它會讓你的衣服立刻黏在身體上，感覺就像是第二層肌膚，而且幾乎無法讓你正常呼吸。對於天生體毛很多的我而言（真不知是一種祝福或是詛咒），只會感覺更悶熱，有好幾次都想「乾脆把它剃光算了」，所以每一次寫信回家時，都會提到「自己就像是一張會走動的蒼蠅紙」，因為感覺所有的東西都會黏上來。

　　別忘記我也是來自一個很炎熱的國家，只是那裡沒那麼潮濕。通常在炎熱的夏天裡，最讓小孩子引頸期盼的一件事就是那滿載著香草或是巧克力冰淇淋甜筒的小汽車，如果你想對自己好一點，甚至可以要求在上面額外灑上巧克力碎片。YA！那真是好吃極了！當我們在外面玩耍、奔跑時，大老遠就可以聽到冰淇淋小汽車那甜美的旋律，那個具有魔力的聲音從遠方傳來時，便告訴我們應該趕快跑回家去跟爸媽要一點零錢來買一支冰淇淋，好把自己從非洲的大太陽下解救出來。

Every foreigner in Taiwan has their own version of this story, but in the end it comes down to the same conclusion: utmost disappointment.

One thing that you'll hear most visitors to the East complain about, is the humidity. As soon as your clothes start sticking onto your body like a second skin and it feels as if you can't breathe properly, it really gets to you. I for one have been blessed/cursed with lots of body hair. Body hair makes you even hotter and there are some days that I just want to shave everything off. Whenever I send an email home, I will say something like: "I'm a walking piece of fly paper again", because it feels that everything just sticks to you.

Don't forget. I'm also from a hot country (with less humidity) and children have one thing to look forward to in the summer. A small ice cream van comes around your neighborhood and serves fresh vanilla and chocolate ice cream in a crisp cone. If you really want to treat yourself, you can even ask for an extra flaky chocolate in the center. Yummy! We would play outside, run around, and in the distance you would hear the sound of sweetness. The ice cream truck would play an enchanted melody in the distance. This would be the sign that you should run into your home and beg your mom for a few coins to have an ice cream.

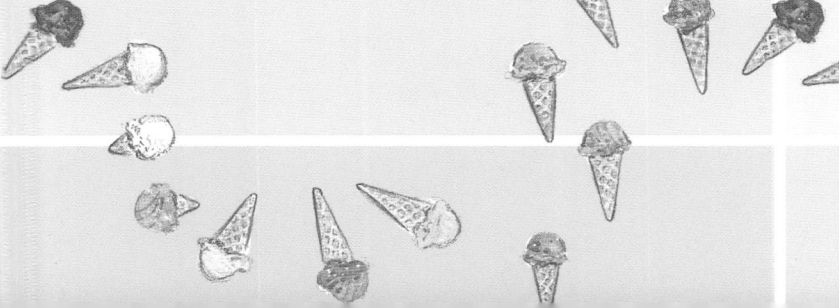

這件事發生在我抵達台灣的第一天。我一邊整理衣服，一邊咒罵著那個冷氣機竟然在六月的盛夏中壞掉了，而那個便宜的電風扇根本也幫不上什麼忙。臉上的汗水就像在比賽一般，一顆緊接著一顆滴落到地板，但這時，我聽見了那個在童年記憶中的甜美旋律，是的，就是那熟悉又甜美的聲音，可以讓我在這炎熱的一天裡好過一些——一台冰淇淋小汽車。

我二話不説馬上甩掉手上的衣服，趕緊找出剛才在機場兑換的新台幣，雖然我還不知道要如何使用它，但至少知道一件事——那就是我現在極需要買一個冰淇淋。

我直衝到樓下屋子的門口，焦急地等待那來自天堂的冰淇淋小汽車，好拯救身處可怕熱浪之中的我，終於在轉角，來了，一台，一台……黃色的……垃圾車！我的下巴幾乎掉到了地上，天啊！怎麼可能！隨著這輛垃圾車的靠近，我不得不接受這個事實，眼睜睜地看著附近的民眾提著大包小包的袋子跑出屋子，並且把它丟進那一輛撥放著我深愛多年的音樂的汽車裡。呃……我被耍了。感覺就像是一個遺失心愛玩具的小男孩，我頭低低的走回屋子裡，一股極度失落感……它來自台灣垃圾車揶揄的聲音。

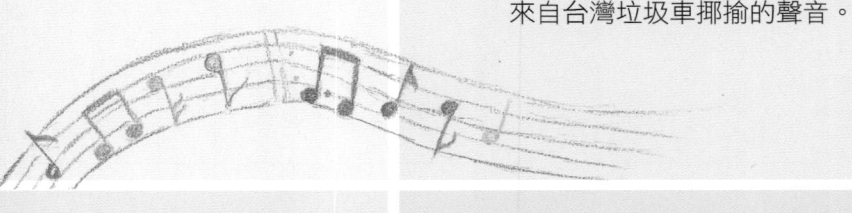

And so it came to pass that I was sitting in Taiwan the first day I arrived here. I unpacked all my clothes and cursed the air conditioner for not working in the middle of June. The cheap fan didn't help much either. The sweat ran down my face as if the drops were competing in a race to get to the floor beneath me. But then… I heard it! The sweet enchanting song from my childhood. The familiar tune that would make this terribly hot day so much better. An ice cream van!!

I threw my clothes off the bed in seconds and looked for my new Taiwan dollars that I'd just exchanged at the airport. I didn't even know how the new money worked, but I knew one thing: I needed an ice cream! Now!

I ran the three flights of stairs to the front of our home. I waited anxiously for the ice cream truck from heaven to save me from this dreadful humidity. And around the corner… came … a yellow …garbage… truck. My jaw almost dropped to the ground. No! This couldn't be! But my fears were soon confirmed as the garbage truck drew closer. People came running out of their homes with bags and threw them into this truck playing the tinkling tune I'd loved for so many years. Foul! I'd been cheated! I felt like a little boy who lost his favorite toy and headed back into the house… defeated by the teasing sound of a Taiwanese garbage truck.

我恨死你了！」的旋律

Trashy song! I hate you!

06

文化衝擊
Culture Shock

玻璃窗裡的白雪公主

如果你問我在台灣，哪一件事帶給我的衝擊最大，並不需要太多的時間，我就能從眾多選項中挑選出來，那就是檳榔美眉。對於很多事都只能悄悄發生在家門裡面，既傳統又保守的東方世界裡，她們就像一片額外的拼圖，顯得那麼格格不入。你也許會期待在下一段路程中，能看到這些在玻璃窗裡近乎全裸的小姐們，但是她們就跟檳榔一樣都是屬於台灣的一部份。在很多國家裡，如此打扮的女生，會讓人立刻想到妓女，但是在台灣的這些女孩子並不是你想像的那麼簡單，她們是有自尊心的。她們看起來很性感，而且沒錯！大部分的時間都只是呆呆的坐在那裡（我很納悶，既然她們有那麼多的時間，為什麼不繼續進修得到更高的學歷？）但諷刺的是，但這些年少未經歷練的漂亮美眉卻販賣著讓我們外國人都害怕得要命的噁心檳榔。不管如何，檳榔美眉真的為台灣創造了一個特有的文化，她們是可愛的，她們讓所有鄉間的道路變得有趣多了。誰能說台灣沒有自己獨特又令人讚嘆的景觀？

Snow white and the 4 glass windows

If you had to personally ask me one thing in Taiwan that I probably found as the biggest culture shock, it doesn't take me long to decide which one of the many 'stand out'. In a predominately conservative society where matters behind closed doors are kept there, the beetel nut girl just doesn't fit into the puzzle very well. Half naked ladies in glass cubes are the last thing you'd expect to see next to the roads, but they are as much part of Taiwan's identity as the beetelnut itself is. In any other country, girls looking like this would immediatlely be labelled as prostitues, but in Taiwan these girls aren't as easy as one would expect. They're proud, they're sexy… and yeah.. they are mostly bored stiff sitting there. (I have wondered though why – since they've got all the time – they don't study to get a better education) Isn't it then also very ironic, that this diamond in the rough actually sells the awful betelnuts that myself and so many other foreigners dread!? But, if there's one thing you should keep, it's the beetelnut girl! Truly creative Taiwan! She's fun and she makes the country roads out of the city worth the long drive. Who says Taiwan doesn't have amazing scenery?!

刺這兒、刺那兒

　　在南非，針灸是件不尋常的事，因為基督教在南非非常具影響力，我更是在這種環境中長大。多數的教會並不贊同針灸，他們認為這會造成邪靈入侵，而就是因為這層緣故，我一直到了來台灣的第二年後才敢去嘗試。我以前的觀念是非常排斥針灸的！有誰會這麼瞎的去乖乖躺在那裡，然後隨便讓一個陌生人用針扎滿全身？有誰會瘋到自願去當針線包？直到有一天，我收起我的蠻橫與無知去看了一位中醫師，我才完全改變我對針灸的看法。

當然，他要先診斷我的身體，就像是彈吉他般地在我的手腕上東摸摸、西按按的。然後他用了好像是算命式的口氣告訴我說我哪裡不對勁，我不敢相信地目瞪口呆的看著他，因為我還沒告訴他隻字片語，他怎麼會知道我的症狀！

他很嚴肅，用結結巴巴的英文告訴我：「我會把你『修理』好！」就在還沒搞清楚狀況的時候，我就像一隻刺蝟般躺在診療室中做治療。回家後的那一晚，我睡得跟豬一樣。而自從那一天起，我便常常去找那位老醫生扎針：「請把我插滿針吧！」

Needle me here.. Needle me there

Acupuncture is not common in my country. South Africa is predominately Christian and I was brought up as one. Most churches condemn acupuncture. They say you open your spirit to bad things. This is why I was in Taiwan for two years before I tried it. I was personally very skeptical about the whole acupuncture idea. Who in their right mind would lie down quietly and allow people to stick needles into them. Why would anyone want to be a human pin cushion? Those were my thoughts, until the day I actually put my pride in my pocket and walked into the doctor's room.

At first he had to diagnose me. He took my wrist and played my veins as if they were guitar strings. The next moment he sounded like a fortune teller and told me exactly what was wrong with me. How could he know all this? I hadn't said a word! I was flabbergasted.

The doctor told me in a bad English accent that he'd 'fix' me. And in seconds I was looking like a porcupine. I've slept like a rock since then and I often go back. Bring on the needles!

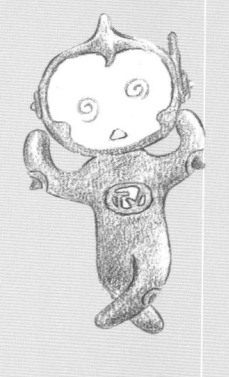

看電視？

你知道嗎？台灣的電視節目非常「熱鬧」，就拿新聞頻道來說吧！那些女主播在電視的某一個小小的角落裡播報新聞。在她的下面有中文字幕，然後是今天的金融資訊和股票指數，再來是下一條新聞提示，然後電視台的Logo又狠狠的占了一個角落。在螢幕的右邊呢，又有一行行的跑馬燈告訴你其他的消息。此時如果剛好有颱風來的話，主播們的頭上還會有下雨的圖片或是動畫！天啊！我只是想知道台灣發生了什麼事，為啥「讀」電視讀到一個頭兩個大。你們是如何辦到的啊！

Reading TV

Taiwanese TV is very interesting. Take a news channel. The lady who's reading the news is in a little square somewhere on the screen. Underneath her you have the words translated into Chinese characters. Below that, you have today's money and markets! Below that is other news. The TV Channel is in one corner and is fairly big. On the right side of the screen more characters are scrolling across the screen, and if there's a typhoon, the news reader even has fake rain falling on her head from the picture above her. Goodness! I've had quite a few headaches trying to figure out what's going on in Taiwan. How do you guys do it?!

典型的台灣新聞頻道，塞得滿滿的中文字

A typical Taiwanese News channel, swarming with Chinese characters.

中式英文

我們喜歡用Chinglish來形容那些翻譯翻得很離譜或是好笑的英文。在台灣和日本還滿多的。有許多人因為不了解其中的意思，也不在意地就亂翻譯，但是對外國朋友來說，有些字的組合真的很好笑了。例如：有一家餐廳的菜單上寫著「鼠條，Frintch Fried」（應該是French Fries）；「汗堡，Han Baoger」（應該是Hamburger）。更別提那些寫在T恤上的英文字了。我曾看過一個老婆婆身上穿的衣服寫了非常好笑的中文字，如果我告訴她，她馬上會心臟病發作，當然同樣的事也發外國人身上，他們也常穿一些自己看不懂但是非常不雅的中國字在身上，因為中文字在國外是非常流行的。

Chinglish

We like to use the term Chinglish when people from a foreign country try to translate their language into English. In Japan and Taiwan Chinglish is quite big. Because many people don't understand what it means, they don't care. But to the foreigners this is very funny. The menus in the restaurants sell "Frintch Fried" and "Han Baoger". And then I'm not even talking about the stuff that we read on people's T-shirts. I've seen old ladies here with slogans on their shirts that would give them a heart-attack if they knew the meaning. Having said that, I'm sure all Taiwanese have a good chuckle when they see what Westerners have written on their clothes. Chinese characters are very popular in Western fashion and we don't know what they mean of course either.

Turd Baby

www.bitobi.com.tw

bitob

2

Sugar Daddy Nice Food
糖菓老爹美食館
美式・意大利餐點・美式調酒・創意飲

稻 (02)

果老爹美食館

鐵路臨時月台開車時
rice List of Temporaty Platf

祝山線 Chushan Line (觀日出 Sunri

預定 第一班 1th	預定 第二班 2th	預定 第三 3th
Bespeak	Bespeak	Bespeak
03:30	03:40	0

另外車次視旅客人數机动

Chinglish:

① 一家飲料店。Turd的意思是一條大便,大便小孩賣的飲料你敢喝嗎?

② Sugar Daddy的英文意思好比是我們所說的「西門町的怪叔叔!」

③ 阿里山的火車時課表上,我發現一個從未看過的新字「Bespeak」,那是什麼意思?而且他們也把第一1st、第二2nd、第三3rd,自動變成超簡單的1th、2th、3th!

④ 在英文裡wheelchair是輪椅的意思,嬰兒車的正確說法應該是Pram。

⑤ 花瓣雨音樂酒吧,「LIVE BLOWING……」現場口交?沒有搞錯吧!

①

④

Public telephone
.嬰兒輪椅借用
Baby wheelchair for
temporaryuse
七.簡介折頁索取
Brief introduction
八.解說導覽
Tour guide

⑤

未 成 年 請

花瓣雨

Music Pub
Live blowing

馬力歐帶你瘋台灣

068

危險七彩調色盤！請戴上太陽眼鏡以策安全！
Dangerously COLORFUL! Please approach with sunglasses!

誰去找個時尚糾察隊！

我最近才聽到這個新名詞，但是這樣的流行時尚，我已經看過不下千百萬次了，他們就是鼎鼎有名的「台妹」。台灣的流行是跟著日本走的，想要成為和日本一樣的流行時尚，但卻又加上自己獨特的創意，於是就造就出來獨一無二的台妹文化。這些迷人的小女生難道不知道這些波爾卡點點早在80年代就退流行了嗎？

你常會在夜市看到這樣一群群的小女生穿著粉紅色的高跟鞋、黑黃條紋的小蜜蜂網襪、鮮綠色的小圓點迷你裙，以及一些寬鬆，但是鮮豔的多層次外套或上衣，這些小女生確定是照了鏡子才出門的嗎？不過在這裡，還是要告訴所有的「台妹」，我還是十分的喜愛妳們的調調。因為妳們給台灣人一種獨一無二的時尚風格，真是太棒了！

Somebody call the fashion police!

I only heard the name a while ago, but I've seen the look a million times. In Taiwan, they're known as the "Tai-Mei". They are everywhere! Striving to be a second Japan, and yet trying to be creative, caused the evolution of the Tai-Mei girl. Most of these lovely young women haven't heard that polka-dots were already out in the 70's. It's so much fun to walk into a bunch of these girls at the night market. Pink pointy shoes, striped black and yellow stockings, a green mini skirt (with polka-dots) and a few loose colorful garments over that. Did that girl actually look nice to herself in the mirror before she attempted the world outside? But to all the Tai-Mei girls out there: We still love you. And good on you for striving for your own unique Taiwanese identity!

現行犯！真是受不了街上這些到處吐紅色墨汁的章魚，檳榔真的很噁心耶！

Caught in the act! Now we know where those red spurts all over the roads in Taiwan come from.

Betelnuts are just... NASTY!

阿彌陀佛！這些人真是太危險了！

My goodness! Look at how dangerous and irresponsible those people are!

媽咪可是花了大筆錢讓你上英文的,去去去!去跟那個阿度仔講英文!

Mommy pays a lot for your classes! Say "hello" to the man! Say "hello".

More Shocks

跟計程車「運將」談政治是無可避免的，不管你是在台灣的哪一個角落。

Avoiding politics in a taxi is almost impossible anywhere on the island!

奇怪吶！台灣人似乎很喜歡放一堆填充娃娃在他們的愛車中。

It's shocking to see how many things some Taiwanese actually have in their cars.

07 回到未來

A Trip to the Future

　　我的座右銘之一便是，在你還沒去嘗試一件事之前，不能妄下斷言。我自認是一個非常開放並且隨時願意去學習、體驗不同文化的人，然而像算命這件對所有台灣人來說是一輩子必定會有的嘗試，而且在這個座小島上竟如此受歡迎，我又怎能錯過？

　　為什麼人們對於未來總是充滿了好奇？我想我們大概都期待有人可以告訴自己未來的一切是多麼順利、很美滿！其實我是一個很「鐵齒」的人，覺得一個人的命運取決於每天、每一刻所下的決定。然而，看見台灣人對於算命如此癡狂，我也決定找個算命仙來看一看未來是如何地飛黃騰達。

　　在一個溼熱的5月傍晚，我來到了這個號稱神準的算命大師住處。找了個地方坐下後，在我的耳邊，仍可聽見外面吵雜的汽車喇叭聲以及鄰近鳥店鳥兒們的聒噪聲，同時，我可以想像這位大師心中的OS：「哪裡來的阿度仔敢來這裡撒野，難道是來踢館不成？」告知了我的來意後（不知大師是否算到我會來找他），大師說我可以問兩個問題，因為我是他的第一個「阿度仔」客人。

How can you judge something, if you haven't tried it at least once? This is one of my mottos in life. I consider myself very open-minded and I am always prepared to learn from different cultures. Fortune telling in Taiwan is a booming business and irrespective of who you are on this island, most Taiwanese would visit someone like this at least once in their lifetime.

Why are we all so fascinated with the future? Because we all just want to actually hear that everything is going to be OK. I don't believe in fortune tellers at all and I honestly believe that one's future basically depends on choices that you make everyday. I was however very interested in why so many people in Taiwan actually do go to these people and I decided to book a 'date' with my own fortune teller.

On a hot humid May evening, I walked into the living area of the man who was going to tell me what the future holds. As I sat down, I could hear the traffic zooming past and hundreds of birds chirping at a nearby bird shop. As I imagined, the man was very interested and confused at the same time due to the fact that he had a foreigner sitting down in front of him. I bet that I was his first foreign customer. He said that he would allow me to ask two questions.

前世今生……紅塵往事，——算盡
Fortune Telling has been with us for ages.

他拿出來了一個小小鐵製的龜殼和6枚古錢，要我丟進去搖一搖，然後把它們倒在一個有4隻小金魚裝飾的小盤子裡。我總共搖了6次，大師則在一旁專心地紀錄下來所有的組合而且在他的筆記本上畫了幾筆，然後，他很嚴肅地看著我說：「盡量問！」

　　在回答問題之前，他會把頭偏向一邊，用鼻子大力的吸了幾下然後回答我的問題，剛開始的時候，我以為他有癲癇的毛病，但我隨即發現這是他和另一度空間「聯絡」的方法。接著我告訴他我寫了一本書，這本書即將在台灣出版，不知是否能賣得好？大師回答說：這書可能不如預期中受歡迎，但也不至於乏人問津（關於這一點，我會證明他是錯的）。同時，大師也告訴我說，我將會在2009年結婚，我老婆會是個紐約客，而且會有兩個可愛的女兒。另外他也提到台灣沒有多少好光景，要趕緊賺錢，並他建議我去大陸沿海的城市發展，那裡比較適合我！

He then showed me a little metal turtle shell and I was told to put the six coins into it, shake it, and throw the coins into a small plate with four blue fish circling it. I did this six times and he ferociously scribbled down a few things on his notepad. He then looked me straight in the eyes and told me to ask my questions. After each question, he made a funny sniff effect with his nose, jerked his head sideways and then gave me an answer. At first I thought he had a kind of epileptic reaction – but soon realised it was the way he 'connected'.

I told him about the book that I'm publishing in Taiwan, and he told me that my book would never reach my expectations. It won't be a big hit. I'm going to prove him wrong. He also told me that I will marry a woman from New York in 2009 and that we'll have two daughters. He said that Taiwan's future is bleak and that there's only a few years left to make money and get out. He suggested I should move to the seaside of China where my future will be best.

説著説著，大師似乎意猶未盡，繼續滔滔不絕地要我多多發問，他説我可以盡量的問，他「有問必答」，誰説「阿度仔」沒有特別的優待啊？所以我告訴他我爸爸在1999年過世了，想知道他在另一個空間過得好不好。這時，看見大師又開始搖頭晃腦用力地用鼻孔吸了一吸！説時遲那時快，大師換了個口音接著説我爸爸過得不錯，只是在等待投胎轉世，我聽後，稍微寬心！但是説實在的，我真的不相信有靈魂投胎轉世的這種説法，看看這個世上每天有多少的新生命誕生，但只有少數的人過世，那要去哪裡找到這麼多新的靈魂來重生呢？這個簡單的問題大家都應該可以答得出來吧！

　　My friendly new psychic was suddenly more than willing to tell me the future. He allowed me to ask as many questions as I wanted to for more than half an hour. Who says foreigners don't get special deals!? I told him about my father who died in 1999 and he connected to the spiritual world with his by now notorious sniff and head jerking. He told me my father is waiting to be reborn and he says that he's fine. I honestly don't believe in rebirth, because there are more people born in this world and fewer who are dying. Where do all the extra spirits come from? It doesn't take a genius in math to figure that one out.

更好玩的事還在後面，這位神奇的大師告訴我說我的家中有兩個「看不見」的訪客，一個老的、一個小的！這兩個「東西」把我的好運都帶走了，他可以幫我處理掉這兩個東西，只要2000元，我想了一下，只要河水不犯井水，每個「人」互不侵犯，我不是很在乎這個問題！

總之，算命還算是蠻有趣的！我並不是要質疑算命仙，只是台灣人都這麼的相信算命才是令我感到不可思議的地方！這是安怎？現在的科技和網路這麼發達，人們為何和這傳統近似迷信的算命這麼緊緊相扣呢？數以百計的情侶在結婚之前算命，請大師算好日子、挑好地方，但有哪一位大師可以告訴我為什麼現在離婚率這麼高？大家不是都去找大師算了最好的日子，同時遵循了所有的傳統習俗來結婚的嗎？我想人心隔肚皮，沒有人摸得透徹！如果有人告訴你說，你9月的時候會十分幸運，我想你一定在9月裡感到幸運，這是因為你相信自己會得到幸運！相信自己，而不是相信在你前面的那一位陌生人。不過綜合說來，我「第一次未來之旅」還蠻不錯的！如果這位大師真的很準，我希望未來的「紐約客」老婆會長得非常的漂亮啦！

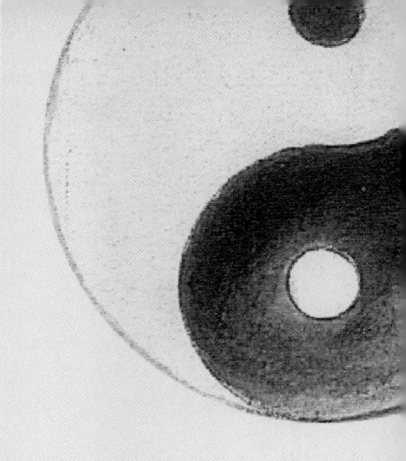

I was also told that my house had two ghosts in the form of an old woman and a young girl. These two were stealing my luck. He would get rid of them for a very small fee of NT$2000. If my house is haunted, I don't really care. I'm happy as long as everyone does their own dishes!

I'm not ridiculing fortune tellers at all, I'm just fascinated that people actually believe them. With all the new knowledge we get from the TV and Internet, how do people still hold on so tightly to these traditions? Hundreds of couples consult them before their marriages and they hear which date is best to marry on and where to get married. Would some fortune teller then tell me why divorces are suddenly such a common occurrence on the island? Didn't those people just do as they were told? I believe that the brain itself is more powerful than any human can fathom. If they tell you that you'll have good luck in September, you probably will, because you believe it so much. The power lies between your ears, not in the man in front of you. With that said, I found the whole trip to my first fortune teller very interesting. And if he's correct, I sure hope my wife in New York is gorgeous!

08

祝你用餐愉快
Bon Appetit

由於以前曾流傳出中國廣東省的人民嗜吃狗肉和貓肉的消息，使得西方人誤認為所有的亞洲人皆是如此。而這也是這本書中所要澄清的，尤其對我而言，壓根兒不會對貓肉感到一絲絲興趣。原先的我真以為在台灣的超市內裡會有斗大的玻璃櫃，裡面展示著尾巴被吊起來的整隻貓肉，或是剛包裝好的大麥町狗肉，所以在來台灣之前我已經做好要吃素的準備。老實說，在南非時，我曾經吃過大象肉和鱷魚肉，不過貓肉……我看還是算了吧！之後當我聽到許多台灣人認為吃狗肉和貓肉對他們來說是件很殘忍、噁心的事之後，我還滿驚訝的。

飲食習慣不同的是兩種文化的差異之一。世界各地很多人喜歡泰國的風味料理，而墨西哥菜及印度菜對喜歡吃辣的人來說，真是無法抵抗。同時，起士愛好者對歐洲料理難以忘懷，而紅肉在南非則不可或缺。

當大部份的人在國外的路上看到那熟悉、斗大的黃色M字時，應該會感到高興。因為身處國外，若對當地的食物感到有所遲疑時，我們還是會選擇到麥當勞享用熟悉的食物。至於要發現台灣美食，真的需要花上一些時間，因為其中一個很重要的原因就是大部份的外國人看不懂中文，

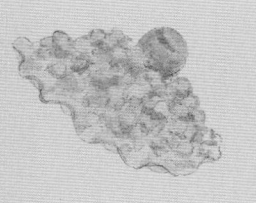

Try as hard as you may, but due to the stories emanating from the Guangdong province in China, everybody in the West believe that ALL Asians eat cats and dogs. And it will take more than just this book to prove otherwise. I was especially not looking forward to eating a kitten. I really thought that Taiwan would have large butcheries with big glass windows displaying a skinned cat hanging from its tail or a chopped up Dalmatian neatly packed in the supermarkets. I was convinced that I would become a vegetarian. I've had elephant and crocodile meat in South Africa, but eating a cat? It was just too much for me. I was really surprised when I later heard, after a while, that the eating of cats and dogs was actually not popular or legal in Taiwan and that many here think it's not normal.

One thing that distinguishes one culture from another is cuisine. People around the world love the exotic flavors of Thai cuisine and for those who like spicier food there is Mexican and Indian. Cheese lovers fancy European dishes, while red meat is popular in South Africa.

Most foreigners are happy to see the big familiar "M" while traveling in a foreign country. When in doubt, McDonalds is still the place for comfort food. It takes a bit of time truly discover the joy of Taiwanese cuisine. Several factors cause us to be wary of what we eat. One huge

因此沒辦法看懂菜單上的方塊字到底寫了什麼。這也就是為什麼在餐廳內，可以看見外國人靠過來看看你在吃什麼。最後，我們（外國人）才能慢慢的學會那些自己吃過，而且非常喜歡的中文菜名，但在這過程中，我們其實已經浪費了許多時間——原本可以拿來享用更多台灣美食的時間。

就我個人而言，水餃和炒飯是我還滿喜歡的料理，而多數餐廳都有的玉米濃湯也相當對味，至於最喜歡的飲料則是木瓜牛奶。台灣的食物雖然剛開始或許會讓你覺得奇怪、不怎麼熟悉，但是只要花上一點點時間來嘗試，很快的就能夠沉浸在各式各樣的驚奇美味當中。

雖然話是這麼說沒錯，但對我們外國人來說，應該還是會有一些奇特的食物會令人退避三舍吧。

reason is that most foreigners don't read Chinese characters, and therefore can't read the menu. This is why you'll probably see a few foreigners leaning towards your table in a restaurant to see what you are having. And eventually we start to learn the names of dishes we've tried and liked. Before long, we are ready to enjoy the variety of flavors that Taiwanese cuisine offers.

Personally, I love dumplings and a good box of fried rice. I also enjoy the delicious corn soups that many restaurants serve and my favorite drink is probably papaya milk. At first Taiwanese food may seem strange and unfamiliar, but with time and effort, one can soon indulge in all sorts of amazing dishes.

Having said that, there will probably always be some food that is just too strange for us to try.

那些看起來好像還不錯吃的樣子！
Those funny white and yellow things look good!

聞聞看

　　當你問那些剛到台灣的外國人，什麼是讓他們最印象深刻的，多數的人大概會異口同聲地說「臭豆腐」。到現在我還記得第一次在夜市跟這位臭先生相遇的時刻。當時我正四處閒晃，好奇的看著那些完全陌生的東西，突然間似乎聞到一股異味。在我還沒準備好之際，那股臭到不行的味道已經冷不防地往我臉上撲了過來，當下我的眼眶開始濕潤，同時覺得頭暈到不行。媽呀！到底是什麼味道這麼嗆又這麼臭啊？我是不介意別人吃臭豆腐，而且事實上我也曾經聽過幾個在台灣的外國朋友們說臭豆腐其實還滿好吃的，但我實在無福消受像這樣的佳餚。

Sniff ... Sniff

　　Ask any foreigner what 'hit' them the hardest after arriving in Taiwan and most of them will probably reply in a chorus "STINKY TOFU". I can remember the first night I met Mr. Stinky at a night market. I was walking around, curious to see all the kinds of things that I didn't recognize. I smelled something strange and suddenly, before I realized what was happening, the scent of stinky tofu smacked me right in the face. My eyes started watering and I felt faint. What on earth could be so strong and smell so bad at the same time? I don't really mind if other people eat it and I've heard of a few foreigners who actually enjoy its taste, but I can't bring myself to eat this "exotic" speciality.

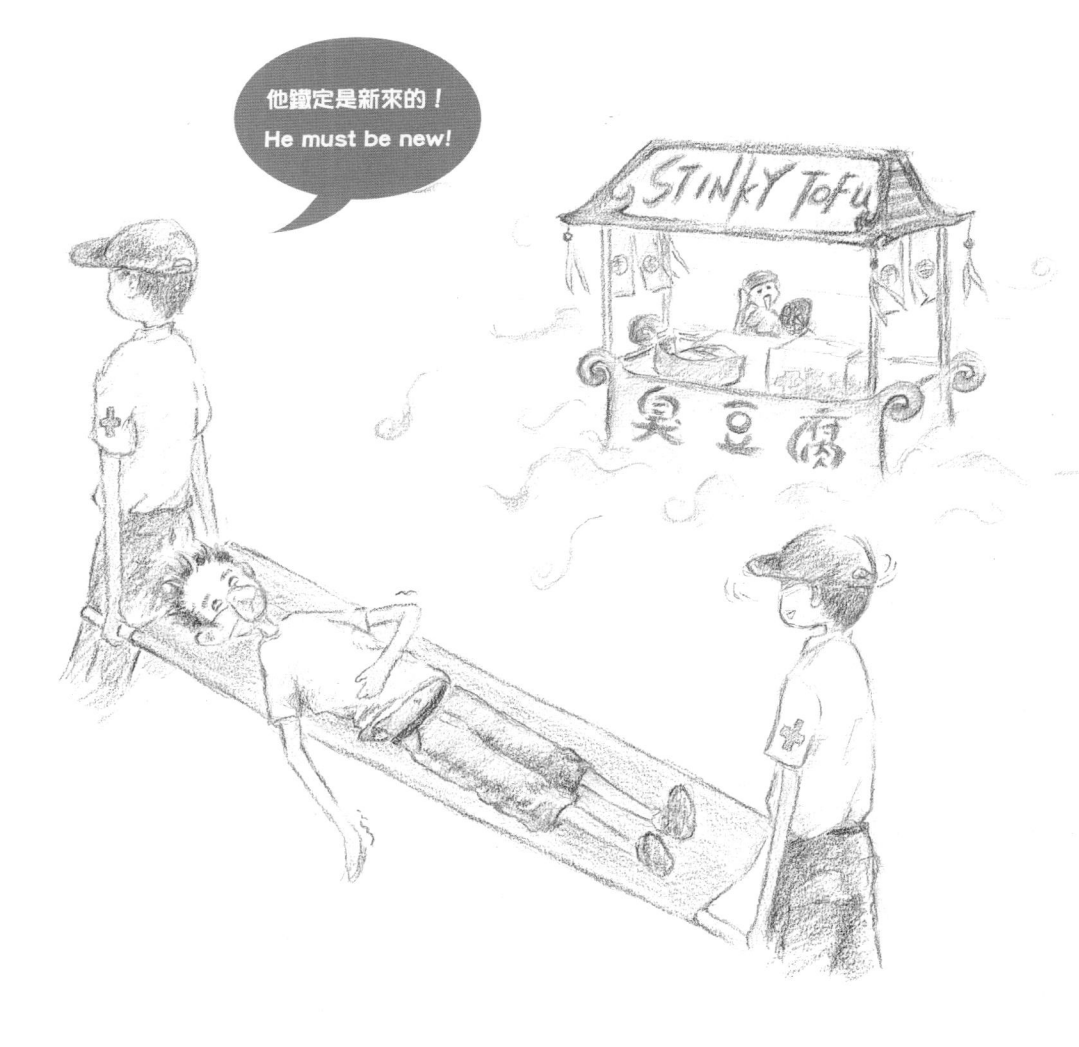

臭豆腐的「臭味」狠狠的衝擊我們的味覺！聞到它，就像被火車撞到。

Stinky Tofu is the one thing that HITS us the hardest when we arrive in Taiwan.

真奇怪！

　　另外一件讓我感到訝異的是，所有的食物都是「完整」上桌，例如整條的魚、整隻雞，或整隻鴨子等等。後來才得知在台灣，這樣的呈現方式原來象徵著「圓滿」。然而對我而言，面對著這些躺在盤子上盯著我瞧的美食時，實在是難以將它們拆解入腹。在西方國家，大家都習慣吃處理好、完全看不出原本的樣子的肉品，因此這真的是得要慢慢適應的。因為在我的家鄉，你完全不會看到整隻雞躺在超市裡等著讓人買走，若真的有，也很少見。

Something fishy

　　Another thing that was quite weird to me was the fact that dishes are usually prepared whole. You'll get a whole fish, a whole chicken or a whole duck on a plate. I learned that in Taiwan this preparation symbolizes unity, yet I find it very difficult to cut an animal while it stares back at me. In the West we're spoiled with meat that doesn't resemble the original animal and this was one thing that I really needed to get used to. At home, you'll seldom, if ever, find a chicken with head and feet in any supermarket. And certainly not hanging from an open rail.

我來付啦！

　　「各付各的」這個詞並不是隨口說說。平常和朋友一起出去吃飯時，西方人都習慣各付各的，通常只有在特殊節日時才會由主人請客。話雖然這麼說，但我的意思並不是指我們喜歡佔別人便宜或者不想請朋友吃飯，而是比較偏向於：「我們一起吃飯吧，不過別爭著付我的帳！」每次我和台灣的朋友一起出去吃飯時，大家總是為了誰要出錢在爭來爭去的。偶爾請一兩次客是沒什麼問題的，不過每次都要請我，也實在太多了吧！所以每當在餐廳看到一群人搶著付帳的時候，就覺得滿好笑的。

I pay!!

　　We also don't say "Go Dutch" for nothing. In the West people tend to pay for the food that they eat and only on special occasions would the host actually pay for everybody. I don't think it's the case that we are greedy and don't want to pay for other people's food, but more like: "Hey... let's have lunch, but let's all pay." I always have so many funny experiences in Taiwan fighting over the bill when I eat out with Taiwanese friends. Treating someone once is fair, but inviting me to dinner a few times and never allowing me to pay is too much! It is fun to go to a restaurant and see the Taiwanese battle it out, over who's paying and who's not.

中國功 〝付〞

中國功夫應該派的上用場！來吧！

Chinese Kung Fu might help paying bills.

雜誌裡寫了什麼？

在我成長的環境裡，情況是這樣子的：每當朋友來我家拜訪時，電視機不會是開著的，取而代之的是大家盡情地聊天。但在台灣的咖啡店卻經常上演著我覺得相當「有趣」的事。一群朋友聚在一起吃午餐，每個人很高興見到彼此，在選了位置坐下來之後，一個人就說了：「唉！今天真忙，好累喔！」同時點餐，接著便走到書報架上選幾本雜誌，然後回到坐位上埋頭讀了起來。有些人則會忙著用手機傳簡訊給朋友，也有人會和其他朋友用手機熱線聊著。等到餐點上來時，大家就開始吃飯，用完餐，再去拿別本雜誌回到座位上繼續看，等到最後喝完飲料，付完錢，大家就鳥獸散了。而當中的全部過程，甚至跟朋友講到話的時間不會超過兩分鐘！這是什麼情況啊？難道你就只會跟其他的朋友說：「我今天跟某某人吃午餐，他過得不錯。」就這樣子嗎？

What's going on in your magazine?

I grew up in a culture where if you have friends coming over, the TV would be turned off and everyone would talk together until they went home. I find the typical coffee shop scene in Taiwan very interesting: There are four friends meeting for lunch. Everyone is happy to see each other. They sit down and say things like: "Wow, I'm tired. Had a busy day!" Then each one orders... walks over to the magazine rack and picks a magazine. Then they return to the table and page through the magazine for a while. Some will send text messages with their cell phones. Some might even phone other friends. Then they'll eat, get a new magazine, drink, stand up, pay the bill and go home. Sometimes I hardly hear any conversation that is longer than two minutes. What's up with that? Do you actually go home and say: "I met John for lunch. He's doing well!"

你是怎麼保持苗條的啊？

哇！我知道西方國家有很多胖子，但有些台灣人真的讓我大吃一驚，尤其是女生！我從來沒在其他國家看過任何一個人即使吃了不少東西，但還可以很瘦的。可是在台灣，這種情況卻屢見不鮮！有時我跟台灣的朋友一起吃晚餐，大概從七點吃到九點吧，然後再到夜市去逛逛。但是，當我們才剛到夜市時，他們竟然又餓了！想當然爾，他們一定會在夜市續攤，吃了又吃。台灣夜市裡的許多小吃是用炸的，也很油，但台灣的朋友就是有辦法維持和木板一樣瘦的身材！你們到底是怎麼辦到的呢？我想很多外國人一定迫切的想知道這個「撇步」吧！

哎呀呀！我好餓喔，我
可以吃掉一頭牛！嘻嘻……
Oh my gosh! I'm so hungry! I could
eat a cow!

Where do you keep all the food?!

Wow! The West is known for obese people, but I stare in amazement at some of the Taiwanese. Especially the girls! I've never met a nation that could eat as often, and yet stay so thin! When I meet Taiwanese friends for dinner, we might eat from say 7pm to 9pm. Then we go to the night market and as soon as we arrive they are hungry again! And before we leave, they might have another snack. Many of Taiwan's dishes are deep fried and contain lots of oil, yet the people manage to stay as thin as planks! How do Taiwanese do that? I know that's one secret foreigners would love to know!

妳給我閉嘴！
Oh shut your trap!

分享即是關心

在南非，我的親朋好友都很親切也非常友善，大家喜歡聚在一起吃飯，享受愉快的氣氛。在一般餐廳裡，通常就只是個人吃著個人的餐點罷了，但遇到特殊節日，我們會在家中圍坐在一起，每個人前面擺著一副餐具，然後大家一同享用桌子中間各式各樣的豐盛佳餚，而若這時你是個素食主義者的話，就相當可惜。在台灣也是如此！大家會點許多的菜，然後放在圓桌中間的轉盤上，一起分享，然後你可以從許多不同的食物當中挑喜歡的來吃。在這樣的餐廳裡，每個人的面前也會擺著一個小碟子、碗筷和杯子，而學習什麼東西要放哪裡也得要花上一些時間，不過這就是好玩的地方。除此之外，對一些西方人來說，學習如何正確的拿筷子也是個新奇的挑戰，而要注意的一點是千萬不要把筷子立著，插在碗飯中間！因為不管是對於祭拜祖先或是神明來說，這都是很不尊重的行為。之前的我不知道有這麼一回事，也因此得了個教訓。

Sharing is caring

Back home we are all very warm and friendly people who love to eat together and be merry. On special occasions we will prepare lots of different dishes and put them in the centre of the table. People will then help themselves and you will have one plate, a knife, a fork and a spoon. Usually when we go to a restaurant, you'll only have your own plate of food. In Taiwanese restaurants, people order many dishes and put them in the middle of the table on a "Lazy Susan" and share the dishes. Too bad if you're a vegetarian. You'll have to pick what you like from the variety. All these restaurants may also have a little saucer, little bowl, a small glass and chopsticks. It takes some time to learn where to put what, but that's part of the fun. Learning how to use chopsticks correctly is also another amusing challenge for some of us. You should also keep in mind not to stick your chopsticks upright in your bowl of rice. I learned this the hard way! I didn't know it was offensive and is disrespectful to the local faith.

09 誤會可大了！
Lost in Translation
– it's inevitable

你可以說他沒知識或者超級大笨蛋，隨便你要怎麼說，但是對第一次來到偉大的東方的旅人來說，我們心中早已勾勒出這裡的人是如何如何，以及在這裡要如何生活，吃啥、住啥等等。

你不知道我必須一而再、再而三地告訴我的所有朋友們，事實上，南非有白種人。因為只要我說自己是從非洲來的，大家就會尖叫地說「你怎麼不是黑人！」非洲並不只有黑人而已！這是大家的誤解！白種人和其他有色人種在那裡已經生活了很多年甚至是好幾世紀了！所以，對於東方以及其他國家，我們也有我們的錯誤認知以及誤會，而且這個誤會可大了。

藉由旅行，以及許多的不同經歷，我了解到彼此都是來自非常不同的世界。我非常驕傲自己是南非人，而且跟典型的歐洲人比起來，或許我與南非的黑人有更多的相同點以及共通之處。每個國家和文化都有他們自己一套的做事標準，也就是因為如此，我們才都是獨一無二的。

Call it lack of education or just pure stupidity. Call it whatever you want, but when anyone comes to the Far East for the first time, we arrive here with some sort of expectation of what the people and the place should be like. What they should eat and how they should live.

I can not even begin to tell you how many people I have had to convince that there are actually white people who live in South Africa. This is simply because the of general misconception that everyone living in Africa is black. Whites and other races have however lived there for many centuries and like many, we too have our misconceptions of the Far East and other places.

Through many experiences and through travel, I've gathered that we are from very different worlds. I am proudly South African and I probably have more in common with one of my country's black people than with a typical white European. Every country and culture has their way of doing things. And that is what makes us all unique.

不同國家中，
你不知道的一些有趣事
情和手勢

But not only do we get lost in translation in Taiwan and South Africa, this is common all over the world. Did you know these interesting things about other countries?

女士優先嗎？

你知道嗎？在南非（以及其他西方國家），我，白人男性，如果在女生之前走進餐廳或是房間是非常不禮貌的。但是在黑人的文化裡，卻完全相反的。他們相信男生先進去是要確定裡頭是否安全，所以男生必須先進餐廳或房間，接著女生才能進去。

Ladies first?

Did you know that in South Africa (and other Western Countries), it's rude for a white male to walk into a room before a woman? It works the opposite for black people. They believe it's necessary to first see if the room is safe and therefore the man should go in first.

先出聲或是後出聲

在一些非洲的文化裡，年紀較大的人要先跟和年紀輕的人問候，以表示他想更進一步了解這位少年仔。但在大多數的西方文化裡，這麼做是不禮貌的。在西方的文化中，年紀輕的要先和年紀長的打招呼，以示尊重。

Speak, or be spoken to

In some African cultures an older man should first greet a younger man to show that he finds him worth the conversation. In most Western cultures this again is considered rude. A younger person should speak to the older one first.

請勿觸摸！

在泰國，決對不可以碰觸或者摸泰國人的頭，甚至將東西從他們的頭上方越過都不行。頭，對於泰國人來說是十分神聖、絕對不可侵犯的。

Don't touch!

One should never touch the head of a Thai or pass an object over their heads because the head is considered very sacred in Thailand.

歌手夏奇拉說：「屁股是不會說謊的！」
Even Shakira says the "Hips don't lie"

老媽

對很多非洲國家的女性同胞來說，有一個又大又肥的屁股是非常光榮和美麗的。因為他們相信屁股越大的女生越會生，而且更有母性的光輝，同時也比較會照顧小孩子。

Big mamma!

It is considered a great honor for woman in many African countries to be fat and to have large bottoms. It is believed that the bigger the woman is, the more potential she has to bare children and the better parental skills she'll have.

是的，我的意思是No！

在保加利亞，點頭表示「不」，而搖頭才是YES。

Yes, I mean... No!

A nod of the head means "no" to a Bulgarian, and shaking the head from side to side means "yes"

Hi，小朋友！

在伊朗，伸手和小朋友握手是向他們的父母表示尊重和致意。但是，豎起大拇指則表示非常下流和粗俗，所以要小心！

Hey kids!

Shaking hands with a child in Iran shows respect toward the parents. The thumbs up sign is considered highly vulgar.

喔咕！我需要升官加薪啦！
I have to work on that promotion!

你能彎多低？

在日本，身體直接接觸較不普遍，所以到今天，鞠躬仍是日本文化的一部分。平常打招呼時，職位較低的人要先鞠躬，彎的角度要大、要低，而且要面對職位高的人，躬鞠得越低越好。如果鞠躬的時間越久且鞠的躬越低，所表示尊敬和誠意則越深。

How low can you go?

In Japan physical contact is still not common. The bow is still used today. The person of lower rank should bow first and lowest. The higher the rank of the person facing you, the lower you bow. The lower the bow and the longer one holds the position, the stronger the indication of respect and sincerity.

請讀我的唇

在菲律賓，他們不用手指來指示方向。菲律賓人會把眼睛瞪大，或是嘟起嘴來告訴你方向在哪裡。

Read my lips

In the Philippines, one should point by shifting your eyes or by pursing your mouth in that direction.

他來自斷背山！

在黎巴嫩，如果你要告訴你的朋友誰誰誰是同志，那就用舌頭舔一下你的小指頭，然後劃過你的眉毛。

He's from Brokeback mountain!

To signal that someone is a homosexual in Lebanon, lick the little finger and brush it across the eyebrow.

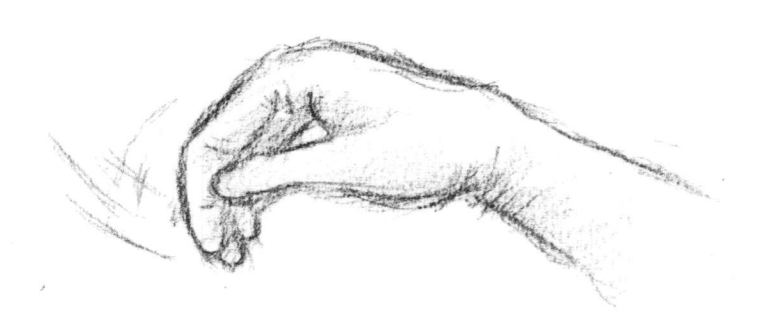

請過來

在諸多亞洲國家中，伸手打招呼或是想請人們過來的手勢是——手掌向下，手指來回劃動。如果是要叫他們的寵物或小朋友，則是手掌向上，手臂朝內來回劃動。但是在西方，這種手勢則是人們在招喚他們的親人及摯愛。

Come over here, please

To beckon someone in many Asian countries, the palm faces downward and the fingers are moved in a scratching motion. Using the arm and hand up, palm toward the face is used only for calling dogs and children. This way is exactly how most people in the West call their loved ones.

哈囉！醒一醒，傻瓜

在智利，手掌向上，然後打開手指是罵某人是笨蛋的意思。

The lights are on, but nobody's home

In Chile, holding the palm upward and then spreading the fingers suggests that someone is stupid.

你好，Salaam

在沙烏地阿拉伯，年長的人會用「Salaam」來打招呼以表示歡迎。男生則以擁抱和互相親吻對方的臉頰來打招呼。但蒙著面紗的婦女則不會主動介紹。

Hello, Saudi style

In Saudi Arabia, elders tend to greet by saying, "Salaam". Men greet with a hug and a cheek kiss. Veiled women are not introduced.

今晚要幹嘛？

在埃及，如果你想問別人要不要跟你「嘿咻」，你可以把雙手的食指並排碰觸一起。這手勢就是詢問另一個人願不願意和你共度春宵。

So, what are you doing tonight?

To ask "Would you sleep with me?", Egyptians tap two index fingers together, side-by-side.

在機器人那向左轉

在南非，所有人都知道什麼是「traffic light」，但南非人很少用這一個字。他們用「ROBOT」這個字來表示紅綠燈，所以有很多從別的國家來的觀光客常搞不懂機器人和紅綠燈的關係。南非人也喜歡在英文中使用「leker」（拉可兒）這個字，在南非話裡「leker」是指東西非常美味或可口的意思。

Turn left at the Robot

South Africans all know what a 'traffic light' is, but the term is seldom used in society. You'll probably hear them using the word "robot". This does confuse people from other countries while traveling. South Africans also love to use the word "lekker" which comes from the Afrikaans word meaning nice, delicious or good.

鈴……鈴……

在阿根廷，如果你的阿根廷朋友覺得你瘋瘋癲癲的，他會告訴你說：「有電話找你。」

Tring Tring

If an Argentinean feels that you are crazy, he might tell you that "you have a telephone call".

音量控制

　　在日本和韓國，大聲的說話或者開心大笑通常是不禮貌的。朝鮮妹和扶桑女都會掩嘴而笑，所以他們大多是咯咯地笑而不是開口大笑。但是在台灣，大聲地說話或者開心大笑通常在餐廳裡是可以接受的。

這家的沙啦看起來好好吃哦！
The salad looks great!

Volume control

Loud talking or laughing is usually avoided by Japanese and Koreans. The women especially, will cover their mouths laughing, resulting in giggling rather than wide open-mouth laughing. In Taiwan however, loudness may be accepted in restaurants.

對啊！對啊！
Oh yeah!

10

聽不懂
Ting Bu Dong

　　「聽不懂」這三個字對於在台灣的外國人來說是滿實用的。對我而言，它有好幾種解釋，可以指「講慢點」、「請用肢體語言告訴我」，或者是「我不懂你說的」。

　　曾經去過許多國家，在眾多的旅遊經驗中也發現了一件事，而且我想許多人也會同意我的看法。中文大概是全世界最難學的語言之一吧！難不是難在音的唸法，而是中文有五種聲調，就是一到四聲，還有輕聲，在西方的語言裡就沒這個問題。例如英文裡的「fish」，不管你慢慢唸、用唱的、用高音講，別人都知道你在講「fish」這個字，然而中文卻是大大的不同。對於剛到台灣的外國人來說，沒學過中文當然不知道會有這檔事。

　　The first few words a foreigner should learn when trying to cope in Taiwan are the helpful words "Ting Bu Dong" which has many translations for me. It can mean: "Talk slower!" or "Please use sign language" or just plain "I don't understand what you're saying!"

　　I've traveled to many places in the world, and many would agree with me. Mandarin is probably one of the five most difficult languages to acquire in your lifetime. It's not so much the pronunciation, but the tones. Western languages have no tones and we can say the word "fish" in all the tones we like… a "fish" stays a "fish" weather sung, said slowly, said at a high pitch or whatever. Chinese obviously doesn't work the same way. Little did the new kid on the block know when he arrived!

寶貝們臉紅了

剛到台灣的時候，我一直很想快點把中文學好，於是我就學到了一句話：「我可以請問你一些問題嗎？」在台灣的前六個月，每當我對女店員這麼說的時候，她們就害羞到不行，不好意思開口跟我說話。有一次，一個台灣朋友在我旁邊的時候，當我開口對女店員說「請問我……」的時候，那位女生馬上臉紅，然後跑走了。當時，我就覺得很奇怪，後來那位台灣朋友就跟我說，「問」如果唸成三聲的話是指「吻」，也就是說，我一直叫別人吻我自己。於是，當下，我也像那些女店員一樣，臉紅到不行。

The blushing babes

I was really keen in learning Chinese as fast as possible and I picked up on the "Please, may I ask you something" phrase. For the first six months in Taiwan I used this sentence and every single girl at a counter blushed and couldn't speak to me. One day my one Taiwanese friend was standing next to me when I said: "Qing wen wo". The girl blushed and ran away. I didn't understand. It was only then that my Taiwanese friend told me that I used 'wen' in the third tone and I was actually saying "Please kiss me!" I blushed just as much as the poor sales girl.

早安！

　　還記得第一次走進家附近的7-Eleven那晚。在踏進去同時，兩位親切的店員便對我說「歡迎光臨（Huan Yin Guang Ling）」。當時我覺得很疑惑，因為聽起來很像「Good morning」，此時我就跟我自己說：「我覺得我來東方國家有兩個使命感：第一，要教好他們的英文；第二，盡可能地幫助這裡的人。」於是，我就向那兩個店員走去，面帶笑容的對他們說：「不！不是Good morning，你應該說Good evening。」這時這兩位店員很緊張，四顆眼睛瞪大地看著我之後，又互看了一下。很明顯地，他們不會說英文，也完全不知道我試著要跟他們表達什麼，最後我拿著飲料，付完帳就離開了。一直到後來我才發現他們並不是說Good morning。當下，我覺得真是糗大了！好丟臉！不過這還好，有時我跟一些女生講話時，因為聲調的關係所鬧出的笑話，比這個還尷尬許多。

Good morning!

　　I can still remember the first night I walked into the 7-Eleven near my home. I came in the doors and two nice people greeted me with a "Huan Yin Guang Ling". I was very confused, because it really sounded to me that they just said "Goo-ood Mor-ning". I said to myself that I'm in the East for a purpose. To teach this nation English and to help everyone. I walked up to the two staff members, smiled and said: "No! It's not 'Good morning'. You should say 'Good e-ve-ning!'". The poor shop assistants looked shaken. They stared at me and then at one another. It was obvious they couldn't speak any English and did not have the faintest idea what I tried to tell them. I eventually bought my drink and left. It was only later that I discovered that they actually didn't say "Good Morning" at all. I was quite embarrassed.

不可以這麼說！

還不只這些呢！當我在教小孩子英文字「槍（gun）」的時候，也意外地學到了髒話。語言就是這麼好玩！不僅一些英文字在中文裡聽起來很好笑，有些中文在其他語言裡聽起來也同樣有趣。例如中文裡的「奶油」在南非其中一種語言裡的意思是非常不雅的，因此到南非時最好別講到這兩個字，以免產生誤解、招來麻煩。甚至台語的「芭樂」在南非的某種語言裡事實上是指「睪丸」呢！所以每次當我在點「一杯芭樂汁」的時候會臉紅不是沒有原因的。但這只是冰山一角，總之，發現語言間的不同以及其代表的意思，還真是有意思呢！

我是小翠！
My name is Tess!

我叫小丸！
Hi, I'm Tickle!

Don't say that!

It's also early in a foreigner's Taiwan adventure that you learn some words should just not be used as I accidentally discovered one day when I told the kids about the 'gun'. How was I supposed to know it sounds like the f… word in Mandarin? But not only some English words sound funny in Chinese. Some Chinese words sound very funny in other languages. The Chinese words for 'milk' and 'butter' in Afrikaans are very rude and one shouldn't use them while traveling there.

In Taiwanese the word for guava (ba la) means 'testicles' in Afrikaans. I always blush when I order "Yi bei ba la zhi!" (One glass of guava juice). But that's just part of the fun. It's amazing to discover the meanings of all these new words.

中文vs.台語

在台灣會説台語是件值得驕傲的事，尤其在南台灣。正因為大家常講台語的關係，所以台語同時深深地影響著中文。這兩種語言都不好學，台語甚至更有著八種不同的聲調！所以見識到語言隨著時間的演化也是很引人入勝的。老實説，若能用清楚而且標準的音調好好唸中文的話，真的滿好聽的，相當希望有一天自己也能説著一口標準、字正腔圓又流利的中文。但不管如何，千萬別把你的母語以及你會的語言放著不用，更別把他們給忘了，因為遺忘某些語言也代表著自己的某一部分流失了！例如南非的一些原住民現在也只會講英語，不會講他們自己的母語了。看到他們獨特文化的某一部份正在慢慢消逝，真的很可惜……

Mandarin vs. Taiwanese

There is a strong pride in speaking Taiwanese, especially in the southern part of the island. Because people use it often, it affects the Mandarin they speak. Both languages are difficult and the fact that Taiwanese has 8 tones doesn't make it too easy to speak either. It's very fascinating to see languages evolve and change through time. I do however think that if Mandarin is spoken with clear tones, it's a beautiful and strong language. I hope I can do that one day. Whatever you do, never stop speaking your mother tongue and the languages you are able to speak. Don't let them go, because by letting them go, you let a little part of who you are behind. Most Indian people in my country only speak English now, and they're losing out on much of their own culture.

現學現賣　Learn some Afrikaans

你知道中文和阿菲利康斯語（南非荷蘭話）有許多發音上的雷同嗎？你可以用以下這些阿菲利康斯語來讓你和南非朋友們溝通喔！

Afrikaans words 阿菲利康斯	Chinese Phonics 中文拼音	Meaning 意義
Hallo	哈囉	Hello 你好
Baie dankie	百啞當ㄅㄧ丶	Thank you very much 非常感謝
Ek hou van jou	æk 後 飯友	I like you 我不喜歡你
Ek hou nie van jou nie	æk後 逆 飯友逆	I don't like you 我喜歡你
Oulike meisie	歐樂客沒ㄙㄧ丶	Nice / cute girl 漂亮的美眉
Oulike ou	歐樂客歐	Nice / cute guy 帥氣的男生

現在，向你的南非友人說以下這句話，他們會告訴你那是什麼意思！

哈囉，友歐樂客等！

11

台灣 VS. 南非
Taiwan vs. South Africa

　　入境隨俗雖然是老生常談，但是對於去過許多國家的我來說，那已是我遵循的常規了！以下這些是我來到台灣後才發現以及學到，與我在南非文化或是生活態度上有差異的地方。

1.

　　我注意到的第一件事是所有建築物的外觀。當我來台灣之後，我幾乎是住在水泥叢林中，放眼所及都是高樓大廈，在南非，我們非常的重視房子的外表美觀，那象徵了某種社會地位，家家戶戶都有很整齊的大草皮以及波光嶙嶙的游泳池，每一棟房子都定期的粉刷，每家的草坪都定期修剪保養，不管你家是家徒四壁或者是億萬富翁，最重要的是要把你自個兒家的門面打理得氣派以及漂亮，這樣才能彰顯你的社會地位。南非是台灣的34倍大，我們有足夠的空間來蓋游泳池以及美麗的花園，在台灣，這剛好是完全相反的！台灣人不會花大把的鈔票來讓房子的外表光鮮亮麗，他們重視的是「內在美」 台灣就是太小了，沒有足夠的地方供人們居住，更不用說是花園泳池了！在南非，大多數的房子都只有一層樓，只有那些有錢人住得起2層樓或是2層樓以上的房子，所以當我看到台灣到處都是5～6層樓，是多麼驚訝及震撼！

They say that if you live in Rome, you have to live like the Romans do. Here are a few things that I had to learn and keep in mind after I arrived in Taiwan:

1.

One of the first things that I noticed in Taiwan, was the state of some of the houses on the outside. As well as the fact that they all reached into the sky. In South Africa, it's essential to have a home that looks beautiful on the outside. Our big grass lawns are trimmed weekly and our swimming pools are sparkling blue. Our homes are painted on the outside on a regular basis and we spend lots of money on our gardens. It doesn't really matter what your home looks like on the inside, as long as it looks great on the outside. In Taiwan the opposite applies. People won't spend thousands of dollars to paint the outside of their apartments just to portray a higher status in life. Taiwan will also easily fit into my country about 34 times, which means we have lots of space for lovely big gardens and swimming pools. Taiwan just doesn't have the space for people to live like this. Back home we tend to build all our homes on ground level and only rich people can afford to have a second floor. It was really interesting to see five and six level homes here – even in the countryside.

2.

　　中國人非常討厭「4」這個數字，因為它和「死」發音相同，而在大多數的西方國家「13」則是非常不吉祥的數字。

　　Number 4 is very unlucky in Chinese, because it sounds like "death". Number 13 is very unlucky in most Western countries.

3.

在南非是不允許任何的高空煙火或是鞭炮的，因為要保護那些野生動物。然而在台灣，我雖然愛死了那些漂亮的高空煙火以及節慶的鞭炮，但是同時也十分心痛，因為人們根本不管那些可憐的動物會因為這些巨大的聲響而四處逃竄。尤其是農曆年的時候！

Having so many precious animals in my country, we need to protect them. Therefore we are not allowed to use any kind of fireworks or bomb crackers. I love the amazing displays of Taiwan's fireworks, but my heart goes out to all the poor animals that have to endure the tremendous noise especially during the Chinese New Year.

4.

在台灣或者是亞洲的其他地方，脫鞋入內是很稀鬆平常的事。但是在南非，我們只有睡覺的時候或者是洗澡時才會脫鞋子，大部分的時間是穿著鞋的，而且，所有的鞋子必須放在櫃子中，否則稍稍不注意，所有的鞋子可能被小偷偷光光！

It's typical to take off your shoes when entering any house in Taiwan and mostly across Asia. Back home we never take off our shoes anywhere in the house. Only in your room before you go to bed or take a bath. All shoes are kept in your closet. They would get stolen outside the front door!

5.

在台灣，親吻和擁抱是夫妻和情侶間的特權，但是在南非，大多數的人（尤其是荷蘭裔的）都是親嘴來打招呼。不管是爸爸媽媽、兄弟姊妹或者是親朋好友，一律親嘴。所以你可以說我們南非人愛玩「親親」，尤其是對剛認識的人，我們絲毫不避諱地展現南非人愛玩「親親和抱抱」的特質。

爹地！我回來囉，我好想你!
Dad! I'm home! I missed you so much!

5.

In Taiwan kissing and hugging are left for married people or lovers. In South Africa, people, (especially those with a Dutch background) kiss their parents, family members and good friends on the mouth. South Africans love hugs and we would probably hug and kiss you just after the first meeting.

微波爐裡有些吃的，功課沒做完不可以看電視！
Your food's in the microwave. No TV until all your homework is done.

6.

　　南非人的個性大多都是直來直往，想說什麼就說什麼、想做什麼就做什麼，非常真性情的人。對於朋友，我們也會很清楚地表達你是否跟我們是同一掛的人，然而台灣人大多是為了要顧全大局而有所保留，所以常有一些灰色地帶，這常常讓我搞不清楚狀況。

機車!你繼續慢慢講，我有事先走了。
You are so loud!　Why don't you just keep
quiet. I don't like you!　Loser!

6.

South African people are usually quite straight forward. We say what we think and you'll know where you stand with us. I find that Taiwanese people generally would rather avoid conflict and confrontation and due to this reason, they don't always speak their minds.

7.

　　南非人愛死烤肉了，沒有一件事是可以比得上在游泳池旁一邊享受著日光浴，一邊烤肉，尤其是看著大塊的牛排在炭火上烤得吱吱作響的樣子，那可真是人生的一大享受呀！不過，在台灣則是完全相反，台灣的烤肉通常只烤一些小肉串、小丸子，你可知道這落差有多大，我得花一些時間來適應。更別提日光浴了，台灣人好像跟太陽有仇一樣，躲太陽躲得遠遠的！深怕太陽會把他們曬成黑人似的。

　　We love barbecues and there is nothing like having HUGE barbecues with thick juicy pieces of steak sizzling on the fire while getting a nice suntan next to the swimming pool. It was quite something to get used to the small little barbecues that are on sale here and that sunbathing is almost considered a Taiwanese 'sin'.

8.

　　在南非，犯罪率是十分高的！我們大多都在10點前就會回到家中，把自己好好的關在家裡直到隔天早上。在台灣則是越夜越美麗！不管多晚，都有人們或者是小朋友在路上走著，我覺得在台灣的每一分、每一秒都相當安全。

　　Because my country has a high crime rate, it's very dangerous to drive around after 10pm in many places. We usually go home early and lock ourselves inside until the next morning. Taiwan is very safe. Children and grown-ups walk around the street until late at night. I have never felt unsafe in all my time here at any hour.

9.

　　台灣的交通我可以滔滔不絕地給他講個三天三夜。我是來自一個公路暴力相當嚴重的國家，沒有人敢停下車來讓你在他們的面前做迴轉的動作，人們只會不停地按喇叭直到你離開他們的視線。給所有的外國人良心的建議——開車或是騎車越像台灣人越好，如果他們不停紅燈，你也學他們不要停，要不然你會被別人撞上！自從我來台灣之後，我的耐心也被他們磨了出來！不管交通如何混亂，我總是有耐心地慢慢來！這也未嘗不是一件好事！

　　Taiwan's traffic. I can go on and on and on about this one. But, I've learned patience since being to Taiwan. I'm from a country where road rage is huge and people won't allow you to make a U-turn in front of them. People will honk their horns and force you off the road. The best advice I have to foreigners who wish to drive in Taiwan, is to drive like the locals as quickly as possible. If they don't stop at a red, don't do it either… or you'll have others driving into you. Since I've lived here, I seem to have patience in traffic no matter where I go. It's a good thing though.

10.

大多數的南非人和非洲人都有一個共通點，那就是「大屁股」，而女生們也都有比其他國家的女生有更傲人的上圍。正因為如此，要找到合適的衣服簡直就是「不可能的任務！」大多數的店家都會告訴我們「喔！你太胖了，沒有你的尺寸」哎喲！就是諸如此類的事令人生氣！照我的身材，在亞洲都得穿XXL的衣服，但是回到南非，我的SIZE只是M的而已。如果有機會你到南非衣服，可能要跑到童裝區去找小朋友的衣服來穿！

呃！老闆說這是超大尺寸的耶！
Urgh! Urgh! It said LARGE! Large for a grasshopper maybe!

10.

South African and African people have one thing in common. We all tend to have big bottoms. The girls also have reasonably large breasts compared to other girls in other countries. Due to this reason, it's almost impossible to get a pair of jeans or clothes that fit us properly. In many shops in Taiwan they just tell us: "You're too fat to fit in our clothes!" Alas, that's just one of those things. I'm reasonably tall and wearing XXL shirts is quite common in the East now. Back home, I usually wear a Medium. The average Taiwanese might find what they're looking for in my country's kiddy section.

哇塞！阿度仔都長的像大象那麼大隻嗎？
These people are like elephants man!

12 生活拼贴
Scrapbook of Memories

My Taiwanese goddaughter, Bella.

我在台灣的乾女兒——貝拉。

Waterfall at Taroko Gorge
太魯閣瀑布

East Coast
東海岸

Kaohsiung Pagodas
高雄左營春秋閣

Taroko Gorgeous
太魯閣國家公園

Green Island Prison
綠島監獄

Touching the future
101大樓

Tainan county: Fire on Water.
台南水火同源

Douliu Buddha
彰化大佛

Care for some tea?
南橫鹿野福鹿茶景點

Tainan Lantern Festival
台南燈節

Green Island
綠島

Christmas Smiles
聖誕節快樂

I'm flying.
跳傘

Forest of Alishan.
阿里山森林遊樂區

Xiao Yeliou
小野柳

Alishan
阿里山

I love Green Island.
我愛綠島！

Guan-zi-ling Mud
關子嶺泥漿溫泉

Shopping in Pingtung.
屏東血拼

Tea Plantations
阿里山隙頂茶園

13 台灣改變了我
How Taiwan has changed me

沒有人有辦法這麼傲慢地說，他絕不會被其他的文化以及國家所改變，你去過的國家或地方越多，你就會越懂得欣賞以及尊敬每一個不同地方的文化。

在我的生命中，台灣就是這麼的特別而且深深的影響了我。

幾年前，我懷抱著理想和使命來到這個島上，我想要賺多一點錢來讓我家裡的生活更好一點，但是我得到的收穫卻遠比想像中的更多。在台灣，她讓我對微小的事物心存感激，她讓我以不同的角度看待這個世界；她讓我從不同的文化中學習到相同處而不只是一昧的排斥，台灣深深的改變了我。

台灣對於我是照單全收，就連我的缺點也是，也因此，我可以充分發揮才能。在南非，我可以好好地隱藏不為人知的缺點，因為我是處在自己所熟悉環境以及所謂的「安全地帶」裡，一旦到一個新的地方或是新的文化中，所謂的「安全地帶」會完全消失，你必須面對真實的自我──不管是好的一面或者是壞的一面。正因為如此，我了解自己不過是個普通人，而且還有許多需要改進以及學習的地方，也因為這個機會，更了解自己。

One could never be as arrogant as to say that you can travel and not be changed by the new world around you. The more one travels, the more respect you get for each and every country.

And in my life, Taiwan has done just that.

I came to this island a few years ago. I came with a dream: I needed to save money and to better my life. I got so much more in return. Taiwan has taught me to appreciate the small things in life. It has taught me to look at the world with different eyes. It has taught me to learn from other cultures, rather than to condemn them. It has touched my true being.

Taiwan has accepted me for who I am. It has given me a chance to show my talents, and to accept my shortcomings. I was always safe in my Western comfort zone. There I could oppress the nasty parts of my personality. Once you are in a new culture, you are out of that comfort zone and you have to face yourself – all the good and unfortunately, all the bad. But by realizing that I'm only human, lacking many things, I have had the opportunity to get to know myself better.

I have done things that I thought I would never ever do. I snorkeled for the first time

我嘗試了許多自己可能從來都不會去做的事，例如：我小時候曾經溺水過，所以對水一直都著很深的恐懼，但是，我把我的第一次浮潛給了台灣，這對一般人來說也許沒有什麼，但對我而言是十分重要的。很巧的是，我媽媽第一次面對她所害怕浮潛的地方，也正是台灣。她今年60歲，跟我一樣非常怕水，2005年，我終於說服她坐飛機來台灣看我，而且帶她去綠島潛水，她直呼棒透了！而我自己甚至還去台東嘗試跳傘！在台灣，我終於了解自己生活的每一天有多麼珍貴；當我回去南非的時候，我感謝從水龍頭接過來的一杯水；當我抬頭看見滿天無邊無際的星空時，不禁驚嘆、感謝，我了解到了家人的重要性，我不需要最棒的車子或是最大的房子來讓我快樂，真正的快樂是來自內心的愉悅以及感謝身邊的小小事物，我想這就像台灣人所說的「吃果子，拜樹頭」——飲水思源……

在台灣學會的另外一件事是——哭！聽起來一點都不浪漫是吧！那是我人生的一大步，在生命的旅程中，我是一個相當自制的人，當我接到南非家裡的電話告訴我說我最親愛的外婆過世了，我回到出租的公寓中關上房門，眼淚從眼框裡流了出來，我了解自己在台灣是多麼的孤單，

Mom's visit 2005
2005年媽咪遊台北

in Taiwan. Not a big deal for some people, but it was for me. I've always been scared of drowning. Ironically enough, Taiwan was the first place where my mom also faced her fear of snorkeling and she did it for the first time in her life at the age of 60. She visited me in 2005.

I even went paragliding near Taitung and I realized in Taiwan how precious every day of my life really is. When I go home to South Africa, and get a glass of drinking water from a tap – I appreciate it. When I see a star-filled sky, I stand in awe. I've come to realize what family is worth to me and I realize that you don't need the best car and the nicest house to be truly happy. All thanks to Taiwan!

Taiwan has taught me how to cry. Doesn't sound too romantic, right? But it was a big step in my life. When I got the call that my dear grandmother had died back home, I was all alone. I went home to my apartment and cried my heart out for the first time in many years. I cried for the first time after losing my father to cancer six years ago. I've learned that it's okay to show emotion. I've shed a tear each (in silence) every time my Taiwanese kids graduated from kindergarten. I was so proud!

My whole life, I've believed that I wasn't destined for a normal life. I was destined to touch

這是第一次我容許自己哭！這是6年前在父親因癌症過世後我第一次流淚，因為我學會了如何釋放情緒。在我幼稚園小朋友的畢業典禮中，我也偷偷地流下男兒淚（在心理面），因為我為他們感到驕傲。

我一直都相信自己不同於一般人，不管我在哪裡、影響我的週遭人、事、物。教英文並不只是為了賺錢，我覺得有比賺錢更重要的任務，在這裡，我影響了許多人的想法和生活態度，為了這個理由，我也努力地去學中文。在我待的第一個學校，我很驚訝的發現很多爸爸媽媽帶小朋友來學校上課，但是沒有人會擁抱一下然後說再見，我知道這是台灣人的習慣，我應該試著接受，但是這對我來說是不可思議的。在南非，我爸爸或媽媽送我去上課時總是會給一個深深的擁抱然後告訴我他們有多愛我，接著才離開，這是支持我每一天生活的動力，所以，我告訴小朋友們要去教他們的爸爸媽媽要多給他們一些擁抱，同時要常告訴小朋友們爸爸媽媽有多愛他們。半年後，幾乎整個學校都做到了。每一個家長送小朋友到學校後，他們大都會親自下車陪小朋友走到校門旁，然後給小朋友一個深深的擁抱，接著才送他們進校園，小朋友神情愉快地步入校園，因為他們感受到爸爸媽媽對他們的關愛。

lives and make my mark wherever my feet would take me. Little did I know as a young boy that I would spend time in a place where all my cool toys came from!

Teaching here has not just been a way to make money. I felt that I had a specific purpose here. I've touched the lives of many too. In one of my first schools, I found it shocking that parents brought their kids to school, and didn't hug them goodbye. I knew I was living in a different culture from my own, but this was just unacceptable to me. My mom or dad always took me to school and gave me a big hug and told me that they loved me. This gave me the will to go on every day. I told my Taiwanese kids that they must teach their mommies and daddies to hug them often and to say to them, "I love you". Within six months I had almost changed that whole school. Every Taiwanese parent who stopped at the gate would get out of their car, bend down on their haunches and hug their precious children. Those kids would walk into the schoolyard with sparkling eyes – because they felt loved!

Taiwan has truly blessed me with many memories and many wonderful friends. Today, as one of many foreigners, I want to use my voice to thank all of you in Taiwan for taking so much care of us. You probably don't hear it as

台灣給了我非常美好的回憶以及許多好朋友。今天，就像許多身在台灣的外國人，我要謝謝台灣的每一個人這麼幫忙和照顧我們，也許你們不常聽到我的感謝，但我還是要謝謝你們讓我在這裡的生活更舒適方便，也讓我更了解你們的傳統，同時也接受我的南非文化。

我希望台灣能夠更堅強，也希望台灣的每一份子都能非常自豪的成為台灣人！政治的影響力也許會扭曲了一些事實，但是他沒辦法改變一個人的心，也無法改變你是誰，也許我的膚色是白色的，但我絕對是你遇見最以身為南非人自豪的南非人。我希望所有的台灣人都能十分堅強的以身為台灣人而驕傲，在我每一次的旅遊之中，都大力推銷台灣有多好，我要告訴全世界，台灣人是多麼好的一個民族，是台灣讓我變成一個更好的人，也因如此，我深深的感謝台灣，永遠感激……

often as you should. Thank you for making my life good here, for showing me your culture and taking the time to get to know mine.

May this nation raise itself up. May every single Taiwanese be proud of who they are and rejoice in the fact that no one can ever take away from you, who you are. Politics can influence lots of things in this world, but politics can't change our hearts. It can't change who we are. I might have a white skin, but I'm one of the proudest Africans you'll ever meet and I pray that Taiwanese would all realize the power they have and stand firm and proud as Taiwanese. I have proudly promoted your country in all my travels. I've taught the naïve world out there what an amazing people you all are. And I have become a better man because of all of you.

And for that, Taiwan, I will always remain thankful…

你也許渺小

但是你己向世界證明

你不可抹滅的地位

你深深地在我心中留下烙印

永遠都是　福爾摩沙

You lie embraced in the Pacific's watery arms. You've intrigued many with your beauty and magnificence. And with all your spectacular sights —from the coast lines to Mount Jade— you've been the center of a feud for so many years. You've struggled for your own identity and embedding your own unique culture. You might be small, but you have proven to be an island that the world will know, and you've left your mark in my heart. FORMOSA you forever will be.

你靜靜的躺在

太平洋深藍的懷裡

深深的令人著迷

你那令人窒息的風采

與引人注目的景色

從海岸到玉山

你身處險惡的世仇對峙中

掙扎於自我意識的認同

與本土文化的深耕

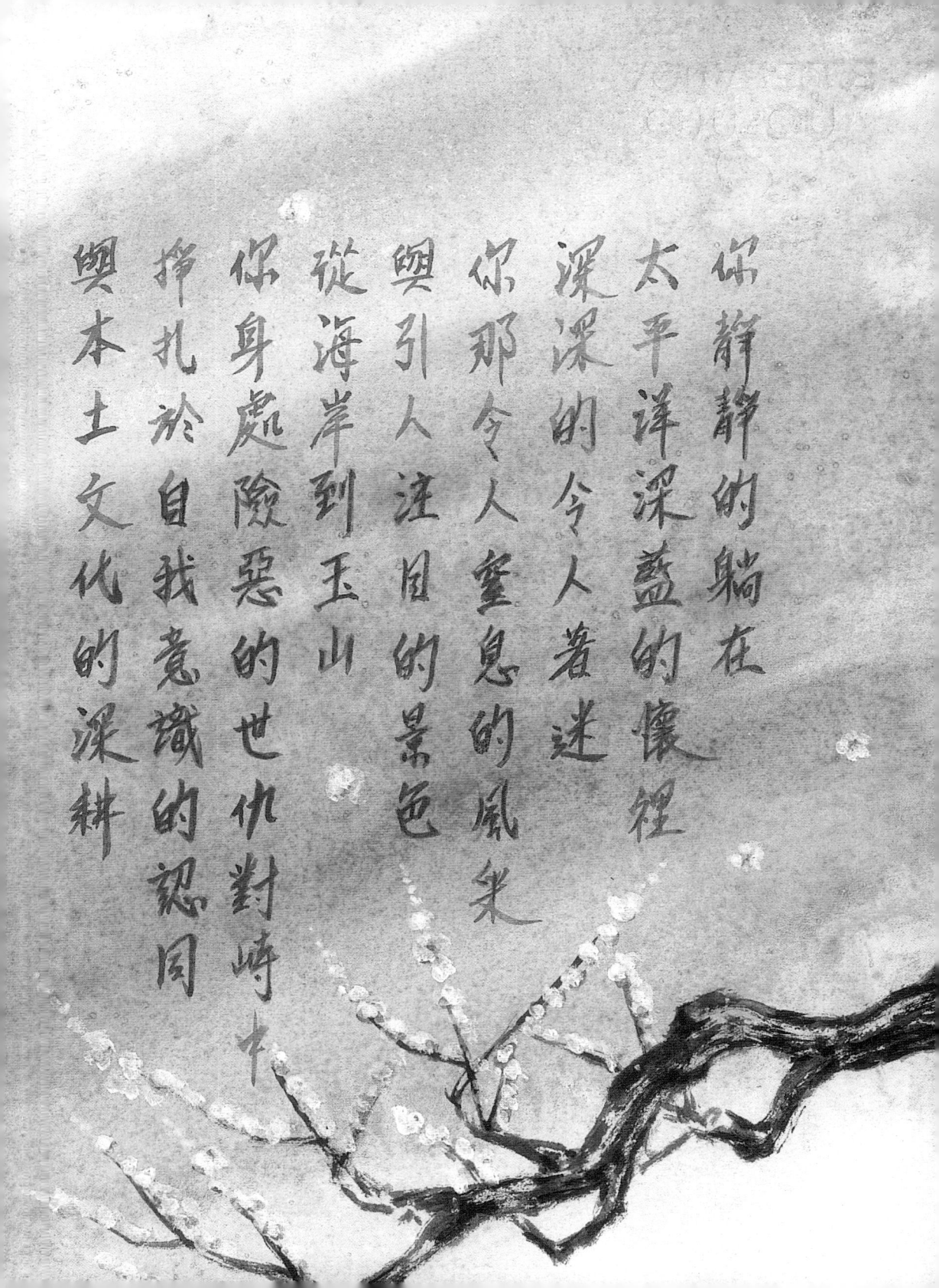

特別感謝 Special thanks

　　我們要特別的感謝這群親愛的狐群狗黨們鼎力的協助，要是沒有他們這本書沒辦法這麼順利的完成的。

　　We would like to especially thank the following people for their devotion in our project. Without you this book could not have been a success.

林志科（Sean Lin）

胡乃馨（Joyce Hu）

李昆樺（Hubert Lee）

吳建明（Chris）

張哲豪

Amanda van Niekerk

Jenny Goossen

Marcelle du Rand

Sven Verelst（史凡）

Terry O'Young

馬力歐帶你瘋台灣

作　者：馬力歐（Marion Erskine）
繪　者：陳怡良

發 行 人：林敬彬
主　編：楊安瑜
編　輯：蔡穎如
美術設計：瑞比特創意設計
出　版：大旗出版　行政院新聞局北市業字第1688號
發　行：大都會文化事業有限公司
　　　　110台北市信義區基隆路一段432號4樓之9
　　　　讀者服務專線：（02）27235216
　　　　讀者服務傳真：（02）27235220
　　　　電子郵件信箱：metro@ms21.hinet.net
　　　　網　　　址：www.metrobook.com.tw
郵政劃撥：14050529 大都會文化事業有限公司
出版日期：2007年1月初版一刷
定　　價：250元

ISBN　10：957-8219-61-X
ISBN　13：978-957-8219-61-8
書　　號：Forth 007

First printed in Taiwan in 2007 by Metropolitan Culture Enterprise Co., Ltd.
4F-9, Double Hero Bldg., 432, Keelung Rd., Sec. 1, Taipei 110, Taiwan
Tel:+886-2-2723-5216　Fax:+886-2-2723-5220
E-mail:metro@ms21.hinet.net
Web-site:www.metrobook.com.tw

Picture Acknowledgment:
P18-3, P.20, P.21, P.23, P.25, © SOUTH AFRICAN TOURISM in South Africa
http://www.southafrica.net

國家圖書館出版品預行編目資料

馬力歐帶你瘋台灣 / 馬力歐（Marion Erskine）著; 陳怡良繪. --
初版. -- 臺北市：大旗出版：大都會文化發行, 2007[民96]

面；公分. -- (Forth ; 7)
ISBN 978-957-8219-61-8 (平裝)

1.台灣－文化 2. 南非－文化
673.24　　　　　　　95023048

大都會運動館 系列

作者：賈斯・哈丁
定價：260元
頁數：全彩96頁
ISBN：986-7651-73-1

Sports 01

野外求生寶典：活命的必要裝備與技能

　　每到夏天，隨著戶外活動的增加，國人發生意外事件的機率也跟著激增，但由於普遍缺乏急救措施的常識和危機應變的處理能力，於是不幸的遺憾就年復一年地在我們周圍發生。然而，意外雖然難以避免，但也不見得那麼可怕，可怕的是我們無知所造成的致命結果。

　　現在不論你是不是個戶外活動的愛好者，這本全彩圖解的「求生寶典」，都將是一本人人必備的救命聖經，讓你在面對始料未及的意外狀況時，自救救人、化險為夷，將危機變成一線生機！

作者：賈斯・哈丁
定價：260元
頁數：全彩96頁
ISBN：986-7651-76-6

Sports 02

攀岩寶典：安全攀登的入門技巧與實用裝備

　　攀岩是一項考驗著體能和心理障礙的極限運動，一方面要承受著地心引力加諸在身上的負荷；另一方面也必須克服人類與生俱來對於高度的恐懼，但種種向極限挑戰的刺激，也正是這種運動的迷人之處。

　　不過，千萬不要輕忽了這項運動的專業性，在踏出你的第一步之前，這本「攀岩寶典」絕對是你邁向頂峰的推手！

中華民國搜救總　　　總隊長　呂正宗
中華民國攀登協會　　理事長　張以青
中華阿魯巴登山協會　理事長　張瀞方
台北市攀岩協會　　　理事長　馬　克

　　　　　　　　　　　　　　　　　　！

FORTH系列

作者：胡菀如
定價：220元
頁數：224頁
ISBN：957-8219-44-X

FORTH 001
印度流浪記 ── 滌盡塵俗的心之旅

一個年輕的台灣女子和旅伴一同前往心中嚮往已久印度，他們沒有設定完善而美好的觀光行程，只是帶著簡單的行囊和年輕驛動的心，深入印度當地並順著機運旅行。在旅程中，他們遇見許多人、事、物，有單純美好，無須言語就能心意相通的淳樸住民；對現狀不滿，不停叨唸、詛咒著萬物的西方人，以及雖然萍水相逢但仍以真誠的心款待他們的森林管理員，甚至是挾文明之力耀武揚威的印度官員……而在與死神擦身而過的經歷中，兩人對生命有了更多的體悟。

FORTH 002
胡同面孔 ── 古都北京的人文旅行地圖

北京五十條胡同，承載多少歷史訊息與文化內涵。尋幽探訪時，逐漸模糊的名人蹤跡，如曹雪芹、龔自珍、蔡元培、魯迅、冰心等，以及胡同的滄桑風貌，都會隨著悸動慢慢浮現心頭。或臨水淡雅、或古樸幽深，縱使已殘破零落，也能窺得雅、韻、樸、幽、影五種深刻的意境。
一條胡同是一個記憶、一種懷念、一份感動，甚或一首詩、一段路、一本書。你準備好帶著這本古都人文旅行地圖，推開時光之門，按圖索驥，用「心」去找尋沈潛於歷史中的感動了嗎？

作者：邱 陽
定價：280元
頁數：192頁
ISBN：957-8219-49-0

作者：Kim Roseberry
定價：240元
頁數：176頁
ISBN：957-8219-52-0

FORTH 003
尋訪失落的香格里拉

人人都在尋找香格里拉。香格里拉彷彿午夜夢迴的懸念，在神話與現實的地平線上遊盪。直到神話被印證，世人就在驚嘆中成為無語的朝聖者陸續湧入。
作者以獨特的理性眼光和感性視角，走進人們嚮往的天堂。那裡沒有塵俗的擾嚷，也不是完美的烏托邦，只有藏民投入飽滿的生命力，展現對大自然的景仰，單純而震撼。

FORTH系列

作者：李宗芳
定價：220元
頁數：256頁
ISBN：957-8219-53-9

FORTH 004
今天不飛 ── 空姐的私旅圖

　　不飛的日子，我酷愛旅行。有時一個人獨行，有時身旁多了一個他，就這樣踏上了異鄉，從日本、美國到法國，然後是西班牙、義大利、愛爾蘭、摩洛哥、喀什米爾。那些異鄉的老街、老房子、老教堂，那些飄著濃郁香氣的甜點舖、美味餐館，還有充滿歡笑的小酒館，多年來就像是許許多多快樂的音符，常在我的腦海中迴盪，教人不沉迷也難……

作者：蕭 瑤
定價：200元
頁數：176頁
ISBN：957-8219-54-7

FORTH 005
紐西蘭奇異國

　　魔戒奇觀，僅是誘人發出驚嘆聲的起點，隨著足跡深入葛雷矛斯、福斯冰河、皇后鎮、但尼丁、基督城、羅托魯瓦、陶波、內皮爾、哈士汀斯、新普里茅斯、懷托摩、奧克蘭等各個特色景點，我的見聞別有洞天，我的感受也多了詩意，多了驚豔，多了辛酸，多了爆笑，甚至多了生死一線的心悸……

大都會文化圖書目錄

◆寵物當家系列

Smart養狗寶典	380元	Smart養貓寶典	380元
貓咪玩具魔法DIY— 讓牠快樂起舞的55種方法	220元	愛犬造型魔法書—讓你的寶貝漂亮一下	260元
漂亮寶貝在你家—寵物流行精品DIY	220元	我的陽光‧我的寶貝—寵物真情物語	220元
我家有隻麝香豬—養豬完全攻略	220元	SMART養狗寶典（平裝版）	250元
生肖星座招財狗	200元	SMART養貓寶典（平裝版）	250元

◆人物誌系列

現代灰姑娘	199元	黛安娜傳	360元
船上的365天	360元	優雅與狂野—威廉王子	260元
走出城堡的王子	160元	殞逝的英格蘭玫瑰	260元
貝克漢與維多利亞—新皇族的真實人生	280元	幸運的孩子— 布希王朝的真實故事	250元
瑪丹娜—流行天后的真實畫像	280元	紅塵歲月—三毛的生命戀歌	250元
風華再現—金庸傳	260元	俠骨柔情—古龍的今生今世	250元
她從海上來—張愛玲情愛傳奇	250元	從間諜到總統—普丁傳奇	250元
脫下斗篷的哈利—丹尼爾‧雷德克里夫	220元	蛻變—章子怡的成長紀實	260元
強尼戴普— 可以狂放叛逆，也可以柔情感性	280元	棋聖 吳清源	280元

◆心靈特區系列

每一片刻都是重生	220元	給大腦洗個澡	220元
成功方與圓—改變一生的處世智慧	220元	轉個彎路更寬	199元
課本上學不到的33條人生經驗	149元	絕對管用的38條職場致勝法則	149元
從窮人進化到富人的29條處事智慧	149元	成長三部曲	299元
心態—成功的人就是和你不一樣	180元	當成功遇見你— 迎向陽光的信心與勇氣	180元
改變，做對的事	180元	智慧沙	199元
課堂上學不到的100條人生經驗	199元		

◆SUCCESS系列

七大狂銷戰略	220元	打造一整年的好業績— 店面經營的72堂課	200元
超級記憶術—改變一生的學習方式	199元	管理的鋼盔— 商戰存活與突圍的25個必勝錦囊	200元

搞什麼行銷—152個商戰關鍵報告	220元	精明人聰明人明白人— 態度決定你的成敗	200元
人脈=錢脈—改變一生的人際關係經營術	180元	週一清晨的領導課	160元
搶救貧窮大作戰の48條絕對法則	220元	搜驚‧搜精‧搜金 —從 Google 的致富傳奇中，你學到了什麼？	199元
絕對中國製造的58個管理智慧	200元	客人在哪裡？— 決定你業績倍增的關鍵細節	200元
殺出紅海—漂亮勝出的104個商戰奇謀	220元	商戰奇謀36計—現代企業生存寶典I	180元
商戰奇謀36計—現代企業生存寶典II	180元	商戰奇謀36計—現代企業生存寶典III	180元
幸福家庭的理財計畫	250元	巨賈定律— 商戰奇謀36計	498元
有錢真好！輕鬆理財的10種態度	200元	創意決定優勢	180元

◆都會健康館系列

秋養生—二十四節氣養生經	220元	春養生—二十四節氣養生經	220元
夏養生—二十四節氣養生經	220元	冬養生—二十四節氣養生經	220元
春夏秋冬養生套書	699元	寒天—０卡路里的健康瘦身新主張	200元
地中海纖體美人湯飲	220元		

◆CHOICE系列

入侵鹿耳門	280元	蒲公英與我一聽我說說畫	220元
入侵鹿耳門（新版）	199元	舊時月色（上輯＋下輯）	各180元
清塘荷韻	280元	飲食男女	200元

◆FORTH系列

印度流浪記—滌盡塵俗的心之旅	220元	胡同面孔—古都北京的人文旅行地圖	280元
尋訪失落的香格里拉	240元	今天不飛—空姐的私旅圖	220元
紐西蘭奇異國	200元	從古都到香格里拉	399元
馬力歐帶你瘋台灣	250元		

◆大旗藏史館

大清皇權遊戲	250元	大清后妃傳奇	250元
大清官宦沉浮	250元	大清才子命運	250元
開國大帝	250元		

◆大都會運動館

野外求生寶典─活命的必要裝備與技能	260元	攀岩寶典─ 　　安全攀登的入門技巧與實用裝備	260元

◆大都會休閒館

賭城大贏家─逢賭必勝祕訣大揭露	240元	旅遊達人─ 　　行遍天下的109個Do & Don't	250元
萬國旗之旅─輕鬆世界通	240元		

◆BEST系列

人脈=錢脈─改變一生的人際關係經營術（典藏精裝版）	199元

◆FOCUS系列

中國誠信報告	250元	中國誠信的背後	250元
誠信─中國誠信報告	250元		

◆禮物書系列

印象花園 梵谷	160元	印象花園 莫內	160元
印象花園 高更	160元	印象花園 竇加	160元
印象花園 雷諾瓦	160元	印象花園 大衛	160元
印象花園 畢卡索	160元	印象花園 達文西	160元
印象花園 米開朗基羅	160元	印象花園 拉斐爾	160元
印象花園 林布蘭特	160元	印象花園 米勒	160元
絮語說相思 情有獨鍾	200元		

◆工商管理系列

二十一世紀新工作浪潮	200元	化危機為轉機	200元
美術工作者設計生涯轉轉彎	200元	攝影工作者快門生涯轉轉彎	200元
企劃工作者動腦生涯轉轉彎	220元	電腦工作者滑鼠生涯轉轉彎	200元
打開視窗說亮話	200元	文字工作者撰錢生活轉轉彎	220元
挑戰極限			320元
30分鐘行動管理百科（九本盒裝套書）			799元
30分鐘教你自我腦內革命	110元	30分鐘教你樹立優質形象	110元
30分鐘教你錢多事少離家近	110元	30分鐘教你創造自我價值	110元

30分鐘教你Smart解決難題	110元	30分鐘教你如何激勵部屬	110元
30分鐘教你掌握優勢談判	110元	30分鐘教你如何快速致富	110元
30分鐘教你提昇溝通技巧	110元		

◆精緻生活系列

女人窺心事	120元	另類費洛蒙	180元
花落	180元		

◆CITY MALL系列

別懷疑！我就是馬克大夫	200元	愛情詭話	170元
唉呀！真尷尬	200元	就是要賴在演藝圈	180元

◆親子教養系列

孩童完全自救寶盒（五書+五卡+四卷錄影帶）	3,490元（特價2,490元）
孩童完全自救手冊一這時候你該怎麼辦（合訂本）	299元
我家小孩愛看書一 Happy學習easy go！　200元	天才少年的5種能力　280元
哇塞！你身上有蟲！一學校忘了買、老師不敢教，史上最髒的教科書	250元

◎關於買書：

1、大都會文化的圖書在全國各書店及誠品、金石堂、何嘉仁、搜主義、敦煌、紀伊國屋、諾
貝爾等連鎖書店均有販售，如欲購買本公司出版品，建議你直接洽詢書店服務人員以節省
您寶貴時間，如果書店已售完，請撥本公司各區經銷商服務專線洽詢。
北部地區：(02)29007288　桃竹苗地區：(03)2128000　中彰投地區：(04)27081282
雲嘉地區：(05)2354380　臺南地區：(06)2642655　高雄地區：(07)3730079
屏東地區：(08)7376441

2、到以下各網路書店購買：
大都會文化網站（http://www.metrobook.com.tw）
博客來網路書店（http://www.books.com.tw）
金石堂網路書店（http://www.kingstone.com.tw）

3、到郵局劃撥：戶名：大都會文化事業有限公司　帳號：14050529

4、親赴大都會文化買書可享8折優惠。

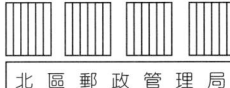

北 區 郵 政 管 理 局
登記證北台字第9125號
免 貼 郵 票

大都會文化事業有限公司
讀者服務部收
110台北市基隆路一段432號4樓之9

大都會文化 讀者服務卡

書名：馬力歐帶你瘋台灣

謝謝您選擇了這本書！期待您的支持與建議，讓我們能有更多聯繫與互動的機會。
日後您將可不定期收到本公司的新書資訊及特惠活動訊息。

A. 您在何時購得本書：_____年_____月_____日

B. 您在何處購得本書：_____書店，位於_____(市、縣)

C. 您從哪裡得知本書的消息：1.□書店 2.□報章雜誌 3.□電台活動 4.□網路資訊

　　5.□書籤宣傳品等 6.□親友介紹 7.□書評 8.□其他_____

D. 您購買本書的動機：（可複選）1.□對主題或內容感興趣 2.□工作需要 3.□生活需要

　　4.□自我進修 5.□內容為流行熱門話題 6.□其他_____

E. 您最喜歡本書的（可複選）：1.□內容題材 2.□字體大小 3.□翻譯文筆 4.□ 封面

　　5.□編排方式 6.□其他

F. 您認為本書的封面：1.□非常出色 2.□普通 3.□毫不起眼 4.□其他_____

G. 您認為本書的編排：1.□非常出色 2.□普通 3.□毫不起眼 4.□其他_____

H. 您通常以哪些方式購書：(可複選)1.□逛書店 2.□書展 3.□劃撥郵購 4.□團體訂購

　　5.□網路購書 6.□其他_____

I. 您希望我們出版哪類書籍：（可複選）

　　1.□旅遊 2.□流行文化 3.□生活休閒 4.□美容保養 5.□散文小品

　　6.□科學新知 7.□藝術音樂 8.□致富理財 9.□工商企管 10.□科幻推理

　　11.□史哲類 12.□勵志傳記 13.□電影小說 14.□語言學習（　語）

　　15.□幽默諧趣 16.□其他_____

J. 您對本書(系)的建議：_____

_____

K. 您對本出版社的建議：_____

_____

讀者小檔案

姓名：_____ 性別：□男 □女 生日：_____年_____月_____日

年齡：□20歲以下□21～30歲□31～40歲□41～50歲□51歲以上

職業：1.□學生 2.□軍公教 3.□大眾傳播 4.□ 服務業 5.□金融業 6.□製造業

　　　7.□資訊業 8.□自由業 9.□家管 10.□退休 11.□其他_____

學歷：□ 國小或以下 □ 國中 □ 高中／高職 □ 大學／大專 □ 研究所以上

通訊地址_____

電話：（Ｈ）_____（Ｏ）_____傳真：_____

行動電話：_____ E-Mail：_____

❖謝謝您購買本書，也歡迎您加入我們的會員，請上大都會網站www.metrobook.com.tw
　登錄您的資料。您將不定期收到最新圖書優惠資訊和電子報。

大旗出版
BANNER PUBLISHING

大旗出版
BANNER PUBLISHING

大旗出版
BANNER PUBLISHING